SANTA FE, CITY OF REFUGE

Praise for *Santa Fe, City of Refuge*

"Get ready to meet a loveable crew of outcasts, stoners, hippies, political junkies, anti-war activists and crazy, bridge players. From nearly being arrested in Yugoslavia by security guards for trying to harm that country's authoritarian leader, to dodging tear gas canisters and police in riot gear on the streets of Chicago in 1968, Wilson's precise and entertaining prose gives readers an exhilarating feel to be at the heart of the era's hotspots: Amsterdam, Paris, Venice, Santa Fe.

"*Santa Fe, City of Refuge*, like the era itself, is tinged with violence, creativity, sex and the feeling that 'anything was possible, anything at all.' I alternatively howled with laughter and seethed with renewed rage with every turn of the page."

—Alan Boye, author of *Holding Stone Hands: On the Trail of the Cheyenne Exodus* and *Tales from the Journey of the Dead: Ten Thousand Years on an American Desert.*

SANTA FE, CITY OF REFUGE

An Improbable Memoir of the Counterculture

James C. Wilson

SUNSTONE
PRESS

SANTA FE

Sunstone books may be purchased for educational, business, or sales promotional use.
For information please write: Special Markets Department, Sunstone Press,
P.O. Box 2321, Santa Fe, New Mexico 87504-2321.
Book and cover design › R. Ahl
Printed on acid-free paper
∞

Library of Congress Cataloging-in-Publication Data
Names: Wilson, James C., 1948- author.
Title: Santa Fe, city of refuge : an improbable memoir of the counterculture
/ by James C. Wilson.
Description: Santa Fe, NM : Sunstone Press, [2019]
Identifiers: LCCN 2019001138 | ISBN 9781632932563 (pbk. : alk. paper)
Subjects: LCSH: Wilson, James C., 1948- | Hippies--United States--Biography.
| Counterculture--New Mexico--Santa Fe. | Santa Fe (N.M.)--Social life and
customs--Anecdotes. | Americans--Europe--Biography. | Wilson, James C.,
1948---Travel--Europe. | Man-woman relationships. | Pacifists--United
States--Biography. | Peace movements--United States--History--20th
century--Anecdotes. | New Left--Anecdotes.
Classification: LCC HQ799.7 .W57 2019 | DDC 306/.1097895609046--dc23
LC record available at https://lccn.loc.gov/2019001138

WWW.SUNSTONEPRESS.COM
SUNSTONE PRESS / POST OFFICE BOX 2321 / SANTA FE, NM 87504-2321 /USA
(505) 988-4418 / ORDERS ONLY (800) 243-5644 / FAX (505) 988-1025

On the 50th Anniversary of the open warfare at the Democratic National Convention in Chicago in August, 1968, and the street battles fought in Paris in May of that year, this book is dedicated to the *Soixant Huitards* in Chicago, Paris, and across Europe. May their idealism survive.

Chantal and the author, Strasbourg, France, 1972 (author's collection).

Contents

Part 1 / Yugoslavia

Pula, Yugoslavia. July 18, 1972

Most mornings we would have been at sunny Veruda Beach by then, swimming and sunbathing on the rocky shore, but on this particular morning we'd taken our time. Chantal was stretched out on the bed and I was just waking up. Both of us were ex-pats hiding out: a French woman running from a bad marriage and a numbing career as a school teacher, and a young American running away from years of working and protesting against the Vietnam War.

Before we could decide on what to do next, get dressed and head to the beach or stay and fool around, we heard the distant sound of a marching band outside and then the unmistakable clatter of a parade coming up the street closer to our rented room. What happened next was my fault, no one to blame but myself, *mea culpa*. Call it bad karma or shitty fate or maybe just the insouciance, the blind stupidity of youth. But I was curious, even slightly amused, by the thought of a marching band in a place as remote as Pula, so I climbed out of bed, groped on the floor for my shorts, and hurried across the room to the open window.

From what I thought was the safety of my second floor window I looked down on a surreal scene: two white limousines surrounded by motorcycles coming up the cobblestone street, moving slowly past the two thousand-year-old Roman coliseum, their windshields reflecting the brilliant white glare of the sun. Ceremonial banners and Yugoslavian flags waved from utility poles along the boulevard, while soldiers carrying automatic rifles hurried to take positions along the sidewalk. In the park across the street a band played a brisk military march. Dozens of people cheered, as if on command. Someone threw flowers as the first limousine drew near.

Then I spotted an old man sitting in the back seat of the second limousine. Wearing a white suit and straw hat, he waved stiffly at the crowd. I recognized him as Marshal Tito, president of what was then the Socialist Federal Republic of Yugoslavia. At the age of 80 he looked feeble and a bit dour, not terribly comfortable with the bright sunshine and the noise of the crowd. I had heard from my landlord that Tito was arriving any day to spend the month of July, as was his habit, at his estate on the nearby island of Brioni, but I had no idea that his visit would generate this much hoopla or that his motorcade would pass by my window.

Something about that gray puffy face and dour expression reminded me of the equally dreary politicians back in the States, political hacks like Richard Nixon and Hubert Humphrey, the very people I was trying to forget. Or was it only my imagination, tripped by the blinding light? To get a better view, I scooted out on the windowsill so that my upper body hung outside, suspended over the sidewalk below. How stupid was that? Instantly everyone identified me as an assassin about to strike down their beloved, or maybe not so beloved, leader. Bystanders began to run and shout, while soldiers pointed their guns at my window. I heard Chantal screaming at me to get inside fast: *"Qu'est ce que tu fais? Tu es completement fou!"*

Not knowing what else to do, I waved stupidly at the crowd, as if they had come out on this beautiful July morning just to see me and were there marching on my behalf. Fortunately, my delusion lasted only a split second before Chantal yanked my arm and saved me from further embarrassment. Still waving, and totally lacking in grace, I fell backward onto the floor, from where I looked up at Chantal, who threw some clothes at me and said, *"Vite!"*

As footsteps rattled on the stairway below our room, I tried to laugh at my predicament. *"J'ai merde!"* was all I could think to say, laughter being my only defense against whatever calamity was about to happen. Or perhaps it was the utter absurdity of the situation that saved me from being terrified. Surely, after Chicago, after years of anti-war protests without getting busted, it was beyond the realm of possibility that I would be arrested in Yugoslavia for attempting to assassinate Marshal Tito. It just wasn't possible, not in the rational world I inhabited, or liked to think I inhabited. No way. This wasn't a Greek tragedy or a Kafka novel, I was a privileged (sort of) American spending an innocent (again, sort of) summer in Europe. When I mentioned Greek tragedy and Kafka to Chantal, who spoke no English except for a couple of slang expressions and some Beatles' songs she knew by heart but would only sing when very drunk, she shook her head in disbelief, as if I had lost my mind. Which, in retrospect, probably wasn't too far from the truth.

Seconds later, a furious pounding on our door brought me back to reality. No way to deny that I was in big trouble. For a moment I considered trying to hide somewhere, under the bed or maybe in the wardrobe, but in the end I came to my senses and went to face the music. Surely this misunderstanding could be explained, since we were all rational creatures, yes? But when Chantal opened the door I saw a mob of soldiers waving their weapons and shouting at my landlord, a tall bald man who, when at home, always wore a sleeveless white T-shirt. My landlord shouted back, but he proved no match for the swarm of angry soldiers in their khaki uniforms and black belts. He raised his arms and pleaded for everyone to stop shouting. I couldn't understand a word, since they were all shouting in Serbo-Croatian. I spoke passable French and a smidgen of Spanish, but that was the limit of my linguistic ability.

Oh fuck, I remember thinking, now we've created an international incident.

But Chantal didn't want to be included. She'd shout *"Completement fou!"* and then flip her wrist in disgust in that endearing way the French have of dismissing everyone and everything with one gesture. She glared at me, big brown eyes and long brown hair flowing, electric in the moment.

Total chaos, until my landlord managed to organize a human translation chain. My landlord was a Croat engineer educated in Germany, so he translated the soldiers' questions from Serbo-Croatian to German, which Chantal translated to French, which I translated to English. Then I responded in French, which Chantal translated to German, which my landlord translated to Serbo-Croatian. Thus I was able to plead my case, even though I had no idea if my Serbo-Croatian answers corresponded to my English answers. I feared that my explanation, and thus my innocence would be lost in translation. The more I talked, the more confused the soldiers became until finally my landlord raised his hand high in the air and declared a truce.

"Arrête!" Chantal said before I could say another word.

The soldier in charge, a big burly man with a neatly pressed uniform and a bushy black moustache, frowned and shook his head skeptically. He wanted to see my passport. Then he wanted to see Chantal's passport. Why was a French woman traveling with an American man in Yugoslavia? he asked my landlord, who in turn asked Chantal, who in turn asked me. I had no idea how to respond, since the term "friends with benefits" didn't exist back then. That set off Chantal, who started cursing. Then my landlord threw up his hands, and he and the soldiers began shouting at each other again. Finally my landlord stood back and pointed at the door, daring them to search our room. The big soldier snorted and brushed past my landlord, accepting the dare. Lucky for me the most incriminating piece of evidence he found was an empty bottle of Slivovitch and a dog-eared copy of Hemingway's *En Avoir ou Pas* that I'd purchased at the corner drugstore, the only book in either French or English I'd found on their book rack, where it had probably remained untouched, and certainly unread, for the past ten or so years.

After searching the room, the big soldier seemed satisfied. He warned me to stay out of the window and then left abruptly, still shaking his head at the crazy American and his equally crazy French companion. Just like that the incident was over, reaffirming at least momentarily my view of a rational universe where people didn't get busted for gawking at parades. I breathed a sigh of relief when I realized I wasn't going to be arrested, incarcerated, and tortured by thugs working for an old man who looked like Richard Nixon or Hubert Humphrey. Apparently they weren't even going to deport me, which meant I could continue as planned with my summer in Yugoslavia, my self-imposed exile from my student activities against the Vietnam War over the last four years. I was one of a wave of young American expatriates, outcasts and freaks mostly, who flocked to Europe in the early 1970s, burned out on politics and alienated from mainstream America. For me, Chicago '68 was the turning point and the 'Days of Rage' that followed Nixon's 'secret' bombing of Cambodia in 1970, when we occupied the administration and ROTC buildings and briefly shut down our university, had been the last straw. But I didn't really consider myself an outcast or freak, only a fellow traveler searching for something I could not yet define, an alternative life or maybe just inspiration, and hoping to have a good time along the way.

But none of that explains how and why I came to be on that windowsill in Pula, Yugoslavia.

Paris, France. August 30, 1971

We met in Paris the previous summer. I'd been living abroad, most recently in Paris, where I'd been staying at a cheap hotel on the Left Bank and spending my afternoons and evenings in cafes near the Sorbonne reading Rimbaud and Baudelaire and practicing my spoken French. On this particular day I checked out of my hotel and carried my backpack all the way to the *Gare de l'Est*, hoping to catch the morning train to Munich, where I intended to meet up with friends. Much to my surprise the early morning train had already left without me. That meant I'd have to wait around for another ten hours for the night train to Munich. My other option was to get in some last minute sight seeing and then come back later, possibly after a light dinner, which seemed like a better choice until I stepped outside into a cold, hard rain. Pissed, I walked back to the waiting room and dug in for the long day's journey into night.

Missing the morning train turned out to be an event that changed my immediate plans and nearly changed my life forever. Because not long after I hunkered down on a bench, in walked a shapely young French woman dragging an oversized suitcase. She glanced around the waiting room, mostly empty except for an elderly couple and a family with small children, noticed me, and quickly sat down beside me. We smiled at each other and, after a few awkward moments, I said, "*Bonjour.*"

"*Bonjour,*" she said. "*Vous êtes Anglais?*"

And with that we were off and running, talking for more than two hours nonstop, aided by a pocket French dictionary I carried with me everywhere. I loved the passion in her voice and the animated way she talked and gestured, not to mention her long brown hair, all very seductive. Her name was Chantal, and she spoke no English, or so she claimed (later I discovered this wasn't entirely true). She explained that she was returning from summer vacation in Spain, heading home to Strasbourg, a city in northeastern France located on the Rhine River directly across from Kehl, Germany. I explained that I was on my way to Munich to meet friends, after which I had absolutely no idea where I was going or what I was going to do. Maybe I'll come to Strasbourg, I said, since it isn't far from Munich. She laughed, amused by my boldness.

When her departure was announced, I helped carry her suitcase to the train. Then we said goodbye on the platform, and for the first time since arriving in Europe I felt bummed out and lonely. It seemed the promise of connection had eluded me again. Not wanting to go back to the empty bench, I wandered around the station for a few minutes. Then, from a distance, I saw Chantal come back to the waiting room looking for me. She paused in the doorway, seeing I wasn't there, unsure of what to do next. As I came up behind her I was suddenly overcome by a feeling of joy. I touched her shoulder, and when she turned, a big smile on her face, I fought hard to resist the urge to kiss her right there in the doorway of the waiting room. Instead, we both laughed.

We spent the last minutes before her train left out on the platform saying goodbye a second time. She gave me her address in Strasbourg, and I promised to write, if not to appear suddenly and uninvited at her door.

After Chantal left the day turned sour, culminating in a nightmarish, all-night train ride to Munich that left me exhausted the next morning. To make matters worse, the friend I'd counted on for a place to stay happened to be sleeping with his jealous, demanding landlady. Not only was his apartment off limits to overnight guests except Fraulein landlady, he was generally not free to socialize except for an occasional, clandestine trip to the Hoffbrau Haus for beer and sausages. Another friend, an earnest earth mother type who had been hitchhiking around Europe that summer, had landed in a youth hostel near the Banhof. Having no other choice, I joined her for a few forgettable days before getting bored with the entire Munich scene. I mean, really, how much beer and sausage can you devour before feeling like a sausage yourself?

So when earth mother decided to hitchhike to Amsterdam, I said why not. Legal drugs and prostitution sounded better than beer and sausage. Earth mother knew her way around hitchhiking, and so we scored a ride almost immediately. Unfortunately, the ride turned out to be a fast-talking middle-aged salesman who for two or three hundred miles argued that the German people knew nothing about Hitler's concentration camps and had no idea about what the Nazis were doing in the years leading up to World War II. What concentration camps? By the time we hit the canals of Amsterdam, both earth mother and I were eager to get away from our driver and his protestations. As a last gesture, a last attempt to win us over to his side, he offered to buy us both a drink, which we declined.

How to describe Amsterdam circa 1971? Most of all I remember the acrid odor of pot choking the air and the hordes of strung-out, bedraggled young people with backpacks standing idly by on street corners or playing their guitars for spare change from passers-by while waiting for their next score: the next fix or toke that would make it all better. The canals stank of urine and sewage, and the sidewalks were littered with peace posters and rock'n'roll flyers announcing upcoming events at the local clubs. By chance, not design, we found ourselves in a permissive youth hostel that tolerated drugs and allowed couples to sleep together if they wanted, and although we didn't want, we still had to listen to other couples wander in at all hours of the night and fuck until they exhausted themselves or their drugs wore off. The all-night traffic, the moaning and screaming, made it virtually impossible to get any sleep.

After a few days of sleep deprivation I'd had enough, so I caught a ferry, this time by myself, from Amsterdam to Harwich, and then took the train to London. In London I stayed with friends for a couple of weeks before deciding what I really needed was a month of rest and relaxation on some quiet, pastoral island. I told my friends I was thinking of going to Ireland, but they suggested I instead go to the Isle of Wight, which was closer and less expensive, just a couple of hours south by train. Maybe I'd inhaled too much Amsterdam air, but their advice seemed sound because my money supply, which had taken me a year to accumulate, was fast disappearing. The small, picturesque Isle of Wight would provide the same quiet place to write or reflect on what I intended to do with my life now that I had pretty much given up on the Revolution.

So the next morning I took the train to Southampton and the ferry to Ryde. Somehow I ended up in Newport, the largest city on the island, staying at what was then the Carlton Hotel. They loved me at the Carlton, since I was one of their few paying guests, although they wished I could have come a year earlier for the Isle of Wight rock festival that had attracted anywhere from six to eight hundred thousand people, much larger than Woodstock, they boasted. All the big acts came to play, including Jimi Hendrix, the Doors, the Who, the Moody Blues, Chicago, Leonard Cohen and Joni Mitchell, even Miles Davis for fuck's sake. "You're a year too late," the desk clerk said when I checked in. "You really missed something," the bartender said when I ordered a drink at the bar. Even the manager sought me out just to apologize for my bad timing. "Sorry old chap, but there's not much going on now. I'm afraid you missed the biggest event in Isle of Wight history."

Maybe it was because they didn't want me to feel left out that they kept playing Joni Mitchell's *Blue* album over their PA system in the hotel lobby and bar. As Mitchell's ex-patriot album, *Blue* included songs like "Carey" and "California" about her sojourn among the "freaks" and "soldiers," most of them young people from the States and Canada, who lived together for a period of time in 1970 near Matalla on the island of Crete. I heard the album so many times that I began to think the songs were uncannily relevant to my situation, even though I was living in a hotel on the evergreen pastoral Isle of Wight, not in a cave on a sunny Greek island in the Mediterranean.

The very next morning, feeling optimistic, I bought some notebooks and a manual typewriter just in case the spirit moved me. It didn't. The only thing I managed to write was a letter to Chantal in Strasbourg. Instead of working on whatever manifesto I intended to write, I spent each and every day hiking around the island, from Carisbrooke Castle, where Charles I was imprisoned, south to Tennyson Down, from where you could watch the waves break against the white cliffs overlooking the English Channel. By night I read Tennyson and Keats, both of whom had been unfortunate enough to live on the Isle of Wight, Tennyson for 50 years and Keats for a few brief days on his way to an early death. When I didn't feel like reading, I drank at the hotel bar. Not a bad life for a man on the run, I suppose, but after a month I was bored out of my mind. I couldn't bear to walk down another picturesque country lane dotted with thatched-roof cottages, nor could I bear to read another word of Tennyson or Keats. The boredom, coupled with the fact that my visa was about to expire, led me to rethink my plans. For the time being anyway, I would have to return to the States.

When I got back to Lincoln my roommate Dennis–who I'd lived with intermittently since 1968 when we were tear-gassed and otherwise abused at the Democratic National Convention in Chicago–handed me a letter from Chantal that had arrived a few days earlier. After reading her letter, I knew immediately what my next move would be. I was heading back to Europe as soon as I could raise the necessary funds. More precisely, I was on my way to Strasbourg, this time invited.

Paris, France. June 4, 1972

At O'Hare, while waiting for my flight to Paris, I overheard a bunch of freaks whooping and hollering in an airport bar. Curious, I ducked into the bar to see what was happening. It turned out that breaking news had just flashed across the TV screen: Black Panther sympathizer Angela Davis had been acquitted of murder, conspiracy, and kidnapping in San Jose, California. My new friends, long-haired freaks dressed in tattered denim, were all drinking beers and toasting Angela Davis, who we considered a political prisoner. I joined the party, hoisting a beer someone handed to me, while across the room a group of young soldiers in uniform, either deploying to Vietnam or returning home, glared at us with a mixture of hate and contempt fixed on their faces. It was yet another angry chance encounter in a disjointed age.

Once my Air France flight landed at Orly, I took the subway into Paris and checked into the Left Bank hotel where I'd been staying the previous year. Since I wasn't due in Strasbourg until the following day, I had some time to wander around the city, ending up later that afternoon in a small café overlooking the *Jardin du Luxenbourg*. Paris looked much different than it had just a year earlier, especially the Latin Quarter where the scars from 1968 Paris Barricades were all but invisible. Most of the graffiti had been either blocked out or erased, including the slogans splashed on walls and buildings to mark the uprising: *"De Gaulle Assasin!" "Oui Usines Occupées!" "Nous Sommes Tous Indésirables!" "Non a la Bureaucratie!" "Pouvoir Populaire!"* and the ubiquitous *"Mai 68."*

Looking out on the ornate, orderly gardens and pool, where small children came to sail sailboats and students from the nearby Sorbonne came to talk philosophy, it hardly seemed possible that four years earlier the Latin Quarter had been the scene of the bloodiest fighting during the May 1968 uprising. In just one night, the night of May 10, French police assaulted some 60 barricades, resulting in serious injuries and hospitalization for nearly 400 people, including 250 police. Days later, after a general strike was called, hundreds of thousands of students and workers seized universities and factories and occupied the streets of Paris. Students demanded educational reform, including freedom of speech and liberalization of access to universities. Workers demanded better wages, benefits, and working conditions. By the end of May an estimated ten million French workers were on strike, paralyzing France. The result? President de Gaulle was voted out of office and subsequent governments undertook the *grands réformes* demanded by the strikers. It was, depending on your politics, a great victory or a great defeat. To me it was a great victory, achieving much more than what we did at the Democratic National Convention in Chicago just three months later.

Taking my time, I ordered a beer and reflected on Chicago and subsequent events. For those of us in the anti-war movement, 1968 had been a grim, depressing year, a year that would define us for the rest of our lives. Starting with the Tet offensive in January, when the Viet Cong attacked nearly every city in South Vietnam, shattering the fiction that the U.S. was winning the war, the year turned even more tragic with the assassinations of Martin Luther King and Robert Kennedy in March and June respectively. By August we were angry, embittered, and ready for the barricades when the Democratic National Convention convened in Chicago to nominate Vice President Hubert Humphrey, even though Humphrey had hardly participated in the primaries that year. Humphrey's coronation was the final insult, as it slammed the door on the peace candidate, Eugene McCarthy, for whom many of my friends and I had worked. But despite the protests and the violence in Chicago, nothing changed. The war continued on as before.

Our wounds continued to fester until Richard Nixon, who'd been elected president in November 1968, bombed and invaded Cambodia in 1970, triggering massive demonstrations and riots across America. That spring, during the Days of Rage, students and faculty shut down hundreds of universities across the country, including my own, where we occupied the ROTC and administration buildings. Events spun out of control at several campuses, especially at Kent State where four students were shot and killed by Ohio National Guard troops.

After the Days of Rage, I effectively dropped out of the antiwar movement. I'd had enough. Years of protests, years of being tear-gassed and beaten, banging our heads against the wall, and for what? Ironically, some of the heaviest fighting of the war occurred on Nixon's watch while he and Henry Kissinger pretended to negotiate with the North Vietnamese at the Paris Peace talks. It was clear that the war had to end soon because it was both unwinnable and too expensive, threatening Johnson's Great Society, but meanwhile the bombing and dying continued under the pretext of peace with honor, as if there could be any honor attached to such a racist colonial war that had become a symbol around the world of superpower arrogance and stupidity.

So I declared a separate peace. I moved on. And yet, despite my stated noninvolvement, a funny thing happened during the spring and summer of 1972. I found myself following the presidential campaign, especially the campaign of Democratic Senator George McGovern. I wasn't terribly fond of McGovern, even though he had inherited the peace coalition that McCarthy had put together four years earlier. McGovern was favored to win the upcoming California primary on June 6, so as I sat at the café overlooking the *Jardin du Luxenbourg*, I kept thinking about where I could get a copy of the English Language *Herald Tribune*.

While I brooded about politics, I'd failed to notice the young woman sitting at the table next to mine. With short dark hair, a delicate nose, and an enigmatic smile, she looked like a '70s version of Audrey Hepburn. She wore a paisley wraparound dress that spilled open in front when she leaned forward to sip her glass of wine or turn a page of the book she was reading. It was very sexy, because when she leaned forward her breasts would pop out of her dress, revealing the shadows of her nipples. Before long I became entranced by those fleeting shadows.

"Hey—are you staring at my boobs?" she asked suddenly, out of the blue, in a French accent.

Embarrassed, I started to deny everything but then had second thoughts. What was the point? She'd caught me red-handed staring at her tits. "How did you know?"

"Because I was staring at you," she said, with a feisty twist at the end, almost a challenge. "Let me guess. You're English...a student at the Sorbonne. So how come I haven't seen you in any of my classes?"

For a split second I considered pretending to be what she wanted me to be: an English student.

"I'm Amelie," she introduced herself.

"James," I said. "Actually, I'm not English or a student at the Sorbonne. I hate to disappoint you, but I'm...I'm an American."

She recoiled in mock horror. "Too bad. I don't like Americans."

"What's wrong with Americans?"

"They're...how shall I say? *Ils sont des cochons!*"

"Pigs? Why are Americans pigs?"

"Because of their brutality! Just look at Vietnam," she shot back. "Look at what you're doing to the Vietnamese and their country!"

Though I knew it was against my best interest, I had to call her on this last statement. The irony was just too obvious to overlook. "Wait a minute. You started it. The French were in Vietnam first, in case you've forgotten. We just made the stupid mistake of trying to finish what the French started."

"Yes, but at least we had the good sense to lose and get out," she said, pretending to pout. "America is too big to lose, so you'll never leave, even though you were never invited in the first place."

Now her expression softened. She looked at me closely. "Too bad. My room is just down the street. We could have been friends, maybe. If you were an English student."

I threw up my hands, helpless. "Why don't we restart our conversation, pretend we just met. This time I'll just tell you I'm an English student studying at the Sorbonne. What do you think?"

She laughed

I watched as she placed a five franc note on the table and grabbed her book, *Les Feux de la Chandaleur*, a popular novel by Catherine Paysan that I'd seen in a book kiosk at Orly.

She walked past my table toward the fountain, then stopped and turned around to face me. "Are you coming?"

S trasbourg, France. June 5, 1972

When I arrived in Strasbourg the next afternoon, I checked into a hotel near the train station and without a moment's hesitation headed for the address Chantal had given me on the *Avenue des Vosges*. I had no idea how I would be received by Chantal's parents and sisters, nor I'll admit did I give it much thought. Spending the summer with Chantal felt like the most natural thing in the world to me, even though we'd only met once, spending a mere two hours together in the *Gar de l'Est*. What can I say? Back in the seventies, romance seemed easier, more casual. Or maybe it was just a sign of my youth. At the age of twenty-three, I felt anything was possible, anything at all.

Chantal's mother answered the door, a small friendly woman with dark hair and a twinkle in her eye. "*Si, si, Chantal est au jardin*," she said, and invited me in. She took me into the kitchen, ordered me to sit down, and poured each of us a glass of Grenadine. "*Vous parlez Francais?*" she asked.

"*Un petit peu.*"

She waved me off. "*Mais non, vous parlez bien!*" This time we both laughed.

I couldn't tell if we were laughing at my linguistic limitations or her ironic comment.

Just then Chantal's father entered the kitchen. Stout, gray, and nearly bald, he looked ten or fifteen years older than his wife. After we introduced ourselves, the father insisted we all have another glass of Grenadine. By this time I was starting to feel lightheaded, a bit drunk, because I hadn't eaten since early that morning. "Uh...Chantal?" I asked. They looked at each other as if they'd never heard of anyone named Chantal. "*Au jardin?*" the father asked. "*Si, si,*" the mother said. "*Allons-y.*"

On the way out she retrieved a bicycle from a storage area off the front hallway, and then we were off, her pushing the bicycle and chatting nonstop, me just trying to keep up. I didn't know what Chantal had told her parents about me, but they were incredibly friendly, especially the mother, who also seemed to have unlimited energy. The *jardin* turned out to be a communal garden, where a number of families had small wooden cabanas and garden plots on which they could grow vegetables of various kinds. Chantal and her two younger sisters, wearing bikinis, were sunbathing on chaises. "*Bonjour, bonjour!*" the mother yelled from across the garden. The younger sisters looked amused, but Chantal turned red when she saw her mother and me marching across the garden. "*Bonjour, James...ça va?*" she said, shaking my hand.

After introductions and some initial awkwardness, the three sisters dressed in the cabana and then all of us walked back to their apartment. The father, looking even kindlier after a few drinks, met us at the front door. *On bois?*" he asked, wanting to return to the bottle of Grenadine. "*Non, il faut manger,*" the mother said, taking us all into the kitchen where she set out a plate of cheese and fruit. Chantal looked at me, rolled her eyes, and began apologizing for the antics of her family. But there was no need to apologize on my account. I was enjoying every moment.

Later, when the father fell asleep snoring in his chair, Chantal and I made our escape. We walked for about an hour before ending up in my hotel room, where we stood in the doorway for a few awkward seconds, then entered. Taking a seat on the bed, she said, "*Raconte-moi ta vie.*" Just like that we'd moved from the formal *vous* to the intimate *tu* form of address. I told her about my family and my anti-war activities and that I was a part-time graduate student taking occasional literature and creative writing classes at my university and that I had no real plan for the future. I threw up my hands. "*Vraiment, je ne sais pas.*"

She laughed, but I don't think she really understood my indecision. Having gone straight through school, from *l'école* to *le lycée*, she knew exactly who and what she was and would always be. Her profession and social position were fixed, forever. Even later, when we knew each other intimately, she could never comprehend my sense of life as an open road, ever-shifting and always changing. She considered this view of life as particularly American, naïve and even shallow. Maybe it was, but I could never stop trying to convince her otherwise.

Sitting on the bed, looking at each other across the mattress, we talked about our still-vague plans to go to Yugoslavia for the summer, which we had formulated in an exchange of letters over the past months. The more we talked, the more apparent it became to both of us that our conversation was an obvious ploy to defuse the sexual tension that we both felt but were determined to ignore. She invited me to stay with her family until we left for Yugoslavia. I could sleep on the day bed/sofa in their living room and eat breakfast and the mid-day meal with them. That way we would be closer—and we would save money for our trip. I said yes, not needing to be convinced.

That evening we went out with a young married couple Chantal knew from her school. The husband drove like a maniac, screeching around corners in a sleek sports car that went much too fast for the narrow, winding streets of Strasbourg. He gave me a quick tour of the city, from the historic city center known as the "*Grande Ile,*" where Strasbourg's famous sandstone Gothic cathedral towered above covered bridges and medieval houses, to the stately buildings housing the European Parliament and Council of Europe on the outskirts of the city.

Eventually we ended up at a pleasant outdoor restaurant where all of us ordered drinks and steak-frites. At first we talked aimlessly about the weather, summer vacations, and other nonthreatening subjects. Then the husband turned to me and asked the big question: Did I like the French? Or to be more exact: Did I, unlike most Americans, like the French? His question hung over the four of us like our tattered table umbrella, which looked as though it were about ready to collapse. I hesitated, taking out my dictionary and searching for just the right word, wanting to be funny and witty and to impress my new friends. Unfortunately, I forgot that irony doesn't translate. "*Oui, j'aime les Francais,*" I said. "*Ils sont odieux...comme les Americains.*"

"Odieux?" Chantal asked.

After a moment's silence, everyone laughed. Sort of.

Trieste, Italy. July 2, 1972

The train from Strasbourg wound its way south through the Swiss and Italian Alps down to the plain of Lombardy, reaching Milan by early afternoon. After hours of mountain chalets and pine forests, we descended happily into an Adriatic landscape with brilliant sunshine and dry air. Since we had over an hour layover, I left Chantal with the bags and headed for the newsstand, hoping to find a copy of the *Herald Tribune*. In Strasbourg I'd tried to keep up with events back home, spending part of every day in the periodicals section of the *Bibliotheque National* or, when I could find a copy of the *Tribune* to buy at one of the local bookstores, reading it on a park bench at the *Place de la Republic* or *Place Gutenberg*. From my reading I knew that George McGovern continued to close in on the Democratic nomination for president, having won 230 of 248 delegates in the New York primary on June 20. More intriguing to me was a news story that had surfaced a couple of days earlier involving five men who had been arrested breaking into Democratic National Headquarters at the Watergate Hotel in Washington, DC, where they had apparently attempted to install eavesdropping equipment. According to anonymous sources, the five men had ties to Richard Nixon's re-election campaign and to the White House.

The station newsstand didn't sell the *Tribune*, and I couldn't find any mention of Watergate or the American presidential campaign in the French daily *Le Monde*, so I gave up and returned to the waiting room, where Chantal had fallen asleep on the bench. I joined her, resting my eyes for a few moments before our train was announced. Once on board the train, we opened our cabin window and let the fresh air and bright sunshine wash away our weariness. From the train we caught glimpses of the Adriatic shimmering in the distance, toward Venice and its magical canals. Two short hours later we found ourselves approaching the *Porto Vecchio* and Trieste's *Centrale* railway station, adjacent to the port. Our spirits buoyed by the crisp air and sunshine, we headed for the nearby *Novo Hotel Impero* and, after checking in and quickly freshening up, walked to the massive *Piazza Unità d'Italia* where we had our choice of outdoor cafes for drinks and dinner.

The long day ended back in our hotel room, where we threw off our clothes and continued the celebration. The next morning Chantal wanted to get an early start exploring Trieste. About the only thing I knew about the history and culture of Trieste was that James Joyce, another exile, had lived there from 1904 until World War I. In fact, Joyce began writing *Ulysses*, his masterpiece, in Trieste, before the war intervened and sent him packing to Zurich, where he sat out the war. Chantal shrugged when I mentioned Joyce, unimpressed by writers in general and English language writers in particular, so we worked out a compromise on how to spend our one day in Trieste. In the morning we hit the tourists sites starting with *Miramare* Castle and the Venice-like *Canal Grande*, where brightly colored gondolas bobbed on the tide. Early morning Trieste was a riot of pastels, from the red gondolas and the pale yellow stone buildings to the washed blue sky. Along the way we learned something about the history of Trieste, which had been annexed by successive empires—Rome, Venice, Habsburg, and the Austro-Hungarian—until finally becoming part of Italy in 1920.

The afternoon belonged to Joyce. After a light lunch at a café overlooking the *Porto Vecchio*, we took a self-guided walking tour of Joyce's Trieste, including one of his favorite cafes, the *Caffe Stella Polare*. We toured several of Joyce's former homes, most of them well marked, and then finished the afternoon by walking through the *Cittavechia*, Trieste's former red-light district, which in Joyce's time boasted several hundred prostitutes and dozens of brothels that Joyce was rumored to frequent on occasion, taking his pleasure where he could find it. In *Ulysses* Joyce transformed the *Cittavechia*, using it as a model for his fictional "*Nighttown*." Where better to end our tour of Trieste than the site of James Joyce's erotic adventures? We were embarking on our own erotic adventures.

P ula, Yugoslavia. July 3, 1972

The next morning we slept in thinking we would have a leisurely travel day. Since it was only 86 km from Trieste to Pula, the bus from Trieste would take at most an hour or two, yes? Once in Pula, we would go directly to the tourist information bureau and find a room to rent for the summer. This way we would have all afternoon to look at rooms. That was the plan, anyway. But when we walked to the station and saw the bus, I knew right away we were in for a long, unpleasant ride. Not only was the bus ancient, with makeshift luggage racks on top, but the people getting on the bus carried bags and baskets filled with bread and produce and other food items. I wouldn't have been surprised if some of those bags had live chickens stuffed inside.

Chantal laughed when she saw the overloaded bus, finding humor in the situation. That lasted about 15 km, until we came to the Yugoslavian border, where uniformed guards directed the bus driver to pull over on the side of the highway. Two burly guards in military uniforms climbed aboard and slowly made their way down the aisle checking passports. When they came to where we were sitting, toward the rear of the bus, they asked for Chantal's passport first, handed it back, and then asked for mine. As soon as they saw the "United States of America" printed on the passport, they turned and stared at me, as if they'd just caught a CIA spy. Even worse, a CIA spy who looked like a hippie! Then they said something in Serbo-Croatian, which I didn't understand. "*Je ne comprend pas,*" I said. "*Je parle anglais ou français, c'est tout.*"

The guards waved me toward the front of the bus.. "Fascist pigs!" I whispered to Chantal. The guards took me off the bus and marched me across the highway into a stone structure, part office and part guard tower. They ordered me to sit in a chair while one of them made a phone call, then a second and a third phone call. Who were they calling? What information did they expect to find?

Ten minutes later I was still being held inside the guard structure while the guards took turns making phone calls. Finally, phone calls finished, one of the guards stamped my passport and then wrote something on the stamped page, officially marking me as a troublemaker or whatever. Then they brought me back to the bus, motioning for me to get back on board. For a moment I was tempted to do something foolish, make a sarcastic remark or a bad joke. "*Non, James, c'est dangereux,*" Chantal said from the back of the bus, sensing that I was about to say something I would regret.

Meanwhile, the other people on the bus were pissed because of the long delay we'd caused and were giving us the evil eye. Even worse, having worked up an appetite while watching all this drama unfold, they opened wide their food baskets and bags of produce and started to eat, so that the entire bus reeked, a combination of odors from a really smelly kitchen and an even smellier barnyard. Stinking to high heaven, we drove off down the highway, stopping at every medieval mountain village on the Istrian Peninsula between Trieste and Pula. I can't remember their names because every dusty little village looked exactly the same: ugly stone houses built on a hilltop, surrounded by a medieval stone wall. And in every village more locals carrying bags and baskets of food climbed aboard the bus, so that now there was standing room only on a bus driving 15 km per hour and stopping every ten minutes to pick up more locals. No one ever seemed to get off the bus, only on.

Five hours later, dying from the heat and the fumes, we rolled into central Pula. "Thank God," I said, already standing up in my seat, stretching my legs and back muscles. I felt like I'd just been released from solitary confinement.

Opening up in front of the bus us we saw the Pula waterfront on our right and a large, well-preserved Roman coliseum on our left. A spectacular sight, if we hadn't been too tired to enjoy it. Once we clawed our way off the bus, through the mob of shoppers and farmers, we took a moment to discuss our plans. Since it was already late, we decided to postpone our search for a room to rent until the following day, when we would be fresh. Instead, we hailed an unmarked taxi and asked to be taken to the nearest hotel. Without speaking, the driver tossed our bags in the trunk and took us down to the waterfront, dropping us off at an ugly, squat building with a military façade and a towering flagpole out front, where two Yugoslav soldiers stood at attention. The structure looked more like a military installation than a hotel.

Inside, the institutional beige lobby was almost completely devoid of furniture and was deserted except for one lone clerk, sitting behind the counter reading a magazine. He looked like a stereotypical Cold War functionary, dressed in an ill-fitting suit and vest, with huge dark-rimmed glasses that made his eyes look like pale specks and with his hair perfectly parted on the side, immaculate. He made us both sign the roster and then said, "Passports you please."

"Oh, I think he means passports if you please," I said.

The clerk shook his head. "No if. Passports you please."

This time we handed over our passports without comment. He checked the passports carefully using a magnifying glass and then scrutinized us from top to bottom, as though deciding whether to admit us into his hotel. Finally, begrudgingly it seemed, he gave back our passports and took us upstairs to a room on the second floor. Even worse than the lobby, the hallway upstairs didn't have a stick of furniture anywhere, not a single chair or table, nothing. When the clerk opened the door to our room, I bit my tongue so as to not say anything about the dreary sight. Nothing but a double bed, a chair, and thick brown curtains on the window that blotted out any rays of sunshine that might have penetrated the institutional gloom pervading the building.

The clerk, keeping to his formality, bowed to us as he left the room, closing the door softly behind him. Clank. Like a jail cell.

I glanced at Chantal.

"*Une nuit, c'est tout!*" she said, shaking her head in disgust.

Later, after resting, we walked down to a cafe on the waterfront, desperate for food and cold beer. We took our time at the café, which served skewered grilled lamb and vegetables with fried potatoes. The food tasted great, maybe because we felt on the verge of starvation, so we continued to order more skewers of lamb and vegetables, more glasses of wine and cold beer.

By midnight we'd reached our limit, so Chantal and I walked back to the hotel, arm in arm. In order to get a key to our room we had to wake the night clerk, who was sound asleep behind the front counter. Then, unable to postpone the inevitable any longer, we returned to the drab, depressing room that in the dark looked even emptier than during the day. We were so tired from the long day that we went to sleep immediately.

Pula, Yugoslavia. July 8, 1972

I woke up to find a naked Chantal curled up beside me, all smiles, as happy as I'd ever seen her. The early morning light flooded our room, making the day seem fresh and full of promise. After our long voyage, we'd arrived in paradise. "I never want to leave Yugoslavia," I said. "You understand? *Jamais depart.*"

"*Tu pense? Jamais?*" Chantal asked, humoring me.

The morning after our intolerable bus ride from Trieste we'd found a sunny, spacious room to rent on Flavijeuska Street, just two blocks from a two thousand year-old Roman coliseum called the Arena. Since then our daily rhythms had settled into a comfortable routine. We spent our days swimming and sunbathing at Veruda Beach. Our nights were spent at the outdoor cafes along the waterfront where, as the night wore on, everyone drank Slivovich and liter bottles of Pivo beer and clapped their hands to the music, folk dances mostly, played by old men with gray beards and Gypsy women with long, flowing skirts. Our days took on a dreamlike quality: slow, leisurely afternoons filled with bright sunshine and lots of exercise, followed by the evening bacchanalia.

Every morning we went next door to a sweet little bakery for bread and coffee. After breakfast I sometimes journeyed by myself down to the waterfront newsstands to look for a *Herald Tribune* or a *Le Monde*. Then, mid to late morning, we would walk to the bus station that provided service to the local beaches, stopping along the way to pick up some fruit and drinks for lunch. The ride to Veruda Beach took less than ten minutes, after which we had to walk in from the highway, winding our way through fields of fragrant sage and juniper.

The path took us past a beachfront café and a row of vacation apartments rented primarily by German tourists, and then looped around to the right through a stand of pine trees and finally down to the rocky shoreline. For privacy we pitched our towels on the rocks overlooking the pebbled beach, from where we could sunbathe in private and still run down and plunge into the cool waves when we became overheated. The mid-summer light, as golden as the light in Venice or Trieste, bathed the craggy shore and distant buildings in washed yellow tones that recalled an antique print of vacationers in Greek or Roman times. Some of the women nearest us went topless, while further down the beach, on an isolated peninsula, a few nudists had created their own colony of brown, naked, well-oiled bodies glistening in the sun.

"*Enlever le haut?*" Chantal asked the first day at Veruda, then shot me a dirty look when I responded: "*Tous.*"

Together we spent the mid-part of every day at Veruda Beach, swimming whenever we needed to cool off, but mostly reading and sunbathing in the luminous Adriatic light. Toward three p.m., when we'd had our fill of the sun and the sea, we'd gather our belongings and walk back up the path to the beach café. By this time the German tourists would be fucking in their rental apartments, with their unmistakably unromantic "Ja...Ja...Ja...Ja...Ja...Ja...Ja...Ja!" echoing across the parking lot, while inside the beach café the English tourists would be enjoying their tea and cakes. We would usually stop for a cold drink, and then catch the bus back to Pula and our room, where we would strip and either fool around in bed for the rest of the afternoon or go sightseeing. I preferred fooling around. Chantal preferred sightseeing.

Unknown to us, Pula possessed many exquisite Roman ruins. As young hedonists, we'd come primarily for the beaches, unaware of Pula's ancient history. Conquered by Rome in 177 B.C., the city became an official Roman colony in 46-45 B.C. Our first stop was the Roman coliseum just down the street from our room. Built in the first century A.D., the Arena was said to be the sixth largest surviving and one of the best preserved coliseums in the world, rivaling the Coliseum in Rome. The Arena was still used for cultural events, as we discovered one evening when we attended a performance of Yugoslavian folk dances. In addition, we toured the Arch of the Sergii, a first-century A.D. triumphal arch, and the Temple of Rome and Augustus, built also in the first century A.D. during the reign of the Roman Emperor Augustus. We also explored two gates that were part of the original wall that surrounded the Roman city: the second-century *Porta Gemina*, and the first-century Gate of Hercules. We hiked around the ruins of Pula's two Roman theaters, and we were told that Pula's original forum, built in the first century B.C., remained the main administrative and legislative center of the city.

At the Archaeological Museum of Istria we were surprised to learn that Pula was first mentioned not by the Romans but by the Greek poet Callimachus in his third century B.C. retelling of the Jason and Medea myth. Callimachus called the city Polai, "A city of Refuge:" "On the Illyrian river the oars came to rest.../ a city was founded: a Greek might have called it 'A City of Refuge' / but in their language they named it Polai."

The Jason and Medea story goes something like this: in order to reclaim his inheritance and throne at Iolcus, Jason first had to travel to Colchis and retrieve the Golden Fleece. Not an easy task, even for a hero of Jason's stature, which is where Medea enters the fray. It seems that Medea, daughter of King Aeetes of Colchis and granddaughter of the sun god Helios, also happened to be an enchantress, a priestess of the goddess Hecate. Medea fell madly in love with Jason and offered to help him perform the tasks required in order to win back the Golden Fleece, but only if he agreed to marry her and take her back to Iolcus. Jason agreed, and so Medea, using her potions and magic charms, helped Jason successfully perform the obligatory tasks, after which the two of them fled Colchis and eventually married and produced two children. (I'll skip over the rest of the story, the unhappily-ever-after ending where Jason betrays Medea by taking a second wife and Medea exacts her revenge by killing the new bride and her two children by Jason before whisking herself away to Athens...etc.) Meanwhile, back at Colchis, the expeditionary force sent in pursuit of Jason failed to overtake him and, ashamed to return home empty-handed, exiled themselves to the Istrian Peninsula. There they founded Polai, their "City of Refuge."

Somehow, however obliquely, the tale seemed to resonate with Chantal and my situation. I was her Jason, her anti-hero lover on his own personal quest for an identity he could live with and she was my Medea, my enchantress, my sun goddess. I'd willingly fallen under her spell here in Pula, my own city of refuge, at least for the summer. I tried not to think about what would happen when summer ended. Would Strasbourg become my permanent city of refuge?

When we had exhausted Pula's Roman ruins, our afternoon sightseeing jaunts became less frequent. We weren't particularly interested in Byzantine and Orthodox churches, and the history of Pula, after the fall of Rome, tended to mimic that of Trieste: Holy Roman Empire, Venetian, Napoleonic, Habsburg, and Austro-Hungarian. The main difference came after World War II, when Yugoslavia became an independent communist country under the rule of Josip Broz Tito, commonly known as Marshal Tito. The least interesting of Pula's tourist sites turned out to be the People's Museum, a dreary cement building dedicated to Tito and his communist revolution.

Come evening we'd hurry down to the waterfront cafes for food and drink: skewers of lamb and pork grilled over open barbecue pits, served with a variety of grilled vegetables, and accompanied by carafes of wine and cold bottles of Pivo beer. The music depended on which graybeards and Gypsy women showed up on any given night, and how sober they were, or weren't. Some of the old bastards played better drunk. Others just fell asleep still clutching their accordions, violins, or whatever. Together the drinks, food, and music made for an intoxicating evening, and we were always happily sated when we left the *bacchanales*, winding our way unsteadily through the dark cobblestone streets of Pula at night.

Invariably, the landlord and his family would be in bed by the time we arrived back at our room. That meant we had the place to ourselves and could enjoy our freedom without fear of being overheard or censored. We didn't have to be quiet, or so we thought. Until one night after sex Chantal got up from our damp bed to go to the bathroom. When she opened our door, she found the adolescent son of our landlord kneeling on the floor where he had been looking through the keyhole, trying his best to get a furtive glimpse of paradise.

We laughed as the kid scurried off into the dark apartment.

Like this, our days passed hypnotically. Exiles, we had no past, no roadmap to anywhere else, no shared vision of the future, either together or apart. Nothing but the here and now, the sweet pleasures of the flesh, the lotus of sun and sex.

Pula, Yugoslavia. July 14, 1972

Today I got lucky. I found a *Herald Tribune* at a newsstand farther down the harbor than I usually walk, across the street from where the large international yachts from places like Venice and Athens were moored. The lead story caught my attention immediately: Senator George McGovern wins the Democratic nomination for president. Impatient for news about the convention, I tried to read the newspaper while standing in the middle of the sidewalk among the hustle and flow of pedestrians.

With a dateline of Miami, Florida, the article reported that McGovern, the peace candidate, had won a slight majority of the convention delegates after his campaign out-maneuvered an anyone-but-McGovern movement launched by Hubert Humphrey and Ed Muskie's forces. The key to victory had come down to an adept parliamentary move that seated McGovern's California delegation, which gave McGovern more than the 1509 delegates he needed to clinch the nomination on the very first ballot. That meant the 1972 presidential election would be a clear choice: Nixon or McGovern, war or peace.

My thoughts were interrupted when a sailor from one of the yachts bumped into me and said something in Serbian that, based on the tone of his voice and the look on his face, could only have been an insult. So I took the paper to the nearest park, where I found an unoccupied bench and reread the story and associated sidebars related to the convention. Apparently rumors were circulating about McGovern's choice of a running mate, Senator Tom Eagleton of Missouri and about what McGovern would really do if elected president. Would he, for example, legalize marijuana as some had speculated?

McGovern had repeatedly promised to pull U.S. troops out of Vietnam within 90 days of taking office, so a McGovern victory, whatever else he did, would mark a momentous change in American life. With the war ended and Nixon out of office, the freaks could come out of hiding. The exiles and draft resisters could come home. For the first time in two years of traveling abroad, I felt homesick, a twinge of something...what was it?...maybe pride or at least a belief in the possibility that America could once again become what it had always claimed to be: a beacon of hope and peace, a defender of justice and freedom. Not the military camp it had devolved into under the leadership of Lyndon Johnson and Richard Nixon.

Would the war really end? It hardly seemed possible after so many years of fighting and dying, 50,000 Americans and one to two million Vietnamese dead. Not to mention the bitter cultural divide, the years of antiwar protests and riots on both sides of the issue. Michael Herr said it best: 'Vietnam was what we had instead of happy childhoods." For my generation, Vietnam WAS our life, at least from 1965 through 1972,

Now, suddenly, there seemed to be hope for a future. Only four years earlier, at the last Democratic National Convention in Chicago, hope seemed to have died in the Michigan Avenue beat-down of antiwar demonstrators that resulted in the National Guard being called in to keep the peace and to protect the protesters from the brutality of the Chicago Police.

Sitting on a park bench, halfway around the world, I couldn't help but reflect on what had happened in Chicago four years earlier.

Chicago, Illinois. August 26, 1968

"Tear gas!" someone shouted.

The people in front of me pounded on trashcans and screamed louder at the police lines on the hill facing us. For a moment we held our ground, crouching behind barricades of picnic tables. It was a few minutes before midnight in Lincoln Park. August 26, 1968.

Tear gas exploded in the grass behind us, then everywhere all at once. Clouds of smoke choked the cool air. I couldn't breath.

Then sirens began to scream. Through the glare of searchlights and smoke I saw waves of uniformed police running down the hill with night-sticks and riot helmets. Immediately the protesters scattered, pushing and shoving to escape the oncoming police.

Then I was running, too. Running through smoke and tear gas toward the street at the edge of the park. Unlike Sunday, the day before, I didn't wait to see what would happen. I heard Larry, my companion, sneezing and coughing as we ran. It was only 400 yards, but it seemed like miles. My nose and throat burned, and my eyes itched with tears. But we made it out of Lincoln Park, slowing to a walk as we entered the intersection, pretending to be innocent bystanders who happened to be in the wrong place at the wrong time. As if there were any innocent bystanders in Chicago during that last week in August 1968. No such thing as innocent, and no such thing as a bystander at that particular time and place. The lines were drawn for everyone to see. On both sides of the barricades we were volunteers in the truest sense of the word.

We walked up the street as fast as we could, still hearing the sirens and the explosions behind us. One block up we found Carl Stokes, the mayor of Cleveland, speaking to a group of blacks who were angry because one black youth had been beaten by police. Stokes tried to keep everyone calm, but he had to withdraw once he realized the sheer numbers of the people flooding the streets. We made it as far as the next intersection before the police arrived. First it was a single squad car stopping in the middle of the intersection in an attempt to block our retreat. But when someone threw a brick and shattered the car's windshield, one of the cops inside jumped out and fired a riot gun into the sky. Instantly, half a dozen police vehicles jammed into the cluttered, smoking intersection, now crisscrossed by flying rocks and tear gas canisters.

By this time the crowd had turned left down Wells Street. We were near the front, occasionally breaking into a run to keep ahead of our pursuers. Behind us people lit fires in trashcans and dumped the burning refuse into the street. Someone with a megaphone was telling us to stay calm and stay together. Not easy to do, under the circumstances. Especially when we saw up ahead a line of paddy wagons blocking our path. What was happening suddenly became clear. We were being herded down the street to wagons that were waiting to take us to the Central Police Station over on Wabash Street. The worst was about to happen, or so it seemed. Anything was better than being arrested. We'd heard too many stories about Central.

I stopped, less than a block from the wagons. I could see the fighting up ahead. Police were beating the protesters and hauling them off to the wagons. Some of the young people tried to fight back, but they couldn't put up much of a fight against night sticks and riot helmets. "Fucking Pig!" one kid screamed as a cop hit him in the shoulder with his club. The kid tried to kick the cop in the groin. The cop hit him again, grabbed his leg, and dragged him off toward the wagons.

The protesters scattered in all directions, trying to get away. Out of instinct I ran between two buildings into a dark, narrow alley. Others followed. Then I heard someone shouting for us to stop. Panic set in. I was so scared that I didn't even slow down when I came to a ten-foot wire fence at the end of the alley. I leaped onto the fence and climbed over the loose strands of barbed wire at the top. When my feet hit the pavement, I took off running. Only when I came out into the light on La Salle Street did I become aware of someone running a few steps behind me.

"Wait for me," Larry said.

In my panic, I'd forgotten Larry.

He pointed to my corduroy sports coat. The barbed wire had ripped the sleeves. One of my hands was bleeding.

As we caught our breath, we heard someone coming down the side street toward La Salle. It was another cop. We took off running, but we might have saved our energy. The cop wasn't interested in us. His target was a photographer taking photos of the melee from a position halfway between Wells and La Salle.

"Press!" the photographer shouted and held out his credentials.

The cop pushed aside his credentials and cracked his night-stick on the man's head. The photographer fell to the sidewalk screaming while the cop smashed his camera.

The screams followed us as we ran down the center of the street. We cut over to State Street, where we slowed to a walk and looked for a hotel lobby or a coffee shop. Someplace to hide. Fortunately, we found an all-night coffee shop before the Chicago police found us. We spent what little remained of the night there, drinking coffee and trying to calm down.

I couldn't get my hands to stop shaking, and I couldn't get the crack of the night stick out of my memory. Not that night, and not the next day when I read in the Chicago newspapers that United States Attorney General Ramsey Clark had ordered the FBI to investigate attacks by Chicago Police on twenty-one news reporters and photographers during the first two days of the convention. I kept hearing that sound: the dull crack of wood striking flesh and bone.

Dawn came at last. Cool and breezy. The wind from Lake Michigan chilled us as we walked back to Lincoln Park to look for our friends, Ben and Dennis. But the park was deserted, we discovered. The protesters were still sleeping in the churches and community centers that had given them shelter for the night. Finding Ben and Dennis in these makeshift shelters would be impossible. We didn't want to think about the other possibility: that they could be in jail. So we gave up the search and headed for my car, a 1962 VW bug, beige, with blue and white McCarthy stickers on the front and rear bumpers, no brakes, and no spare tire. The spare had been stolen Sunday, the day we arrived in Chicago.

No brakes and no spare, it didn't matter at the time. I drove that VW bug all the way to Evanston, where the four of us were staying during convention week at the home of a friend of Larry's family. Ben and Dennis were waiting for us. They had taken a taxi from downtown Chicago. The ride had cost them twelve dollars, a considerable sum of money in 1968.

So there we were staying in suburban Evanston, irony of ironies, commuting by taxi to the riots. Four middle class kids, college students. All of us had done volunteer work for the McCarthy and Kennedy campaigns. Like most of the protesters who showed up in Chicago that last week in August, we had come to register our discontent. We had no great plan to disrupt the Democratic National Convention or anything else. But we wanted to be there, to make our dissatisfaction known. Sure, some of the protesters were organized. Groups like Jerry Rubin's Youth International Party, Tom Hayden's Students for a Democratic Society, and David Dellinger's National Mobilization Committee to End the War in Vietnam had actual plans to confront the Chicago Police and march on the International Amphitheater, where the convention was being held. But for every Jerry Rubin, there were a hundred other young people from college campuses across America who made the pilgrimage to Chicago without any plan of action whatsoever.

Let's not pretend, though. All of us came to raise hell, there was never any doubt about that. We were angry about everything, from America's mindless materialism to its repressive Puritan culture and authoritarian government. Most of all, we were angry at Lyndon Johnson's stinking little war in Vietnam. He might not have started it, but LBJ made it his macho own with all his bravado and barroom talk about how he would have Ho Chi Minh's "balls." And we were angry at Hubert Humphrey, Johnson's vice president and chief apologist, who was about to be nominated for president by the patriarchs of the Democratic Party.

It was generational genocide, a Greek tragedy where fathers devoured their own sons. And for what? So that a few old men in Washington could save face? Not good enough. Not for us anyway. We wanted an end to the murderous patriarchy.

So we came to Chicago. We congregated in Lincoln Park, where many of the protesters planned to sleep in tents and sleeping bags. But Mayor

Daley insisted on his eleven p.m. curfew. Everyone had to be out of the park by eleven. And when they weren't, Daley sent in his boys, Chicago's finest, in full riot gear. My God, they were a sight, with their helmets and night sticks and tear gas guns. They removed their badges before joining the fun, not wanting to be recognized, these sons, husbands, and fathers of Chicago. They didn't want the camera to identify them, to connect their names with these acts. No, they wanted their pleasure anonymously. And it was pleasure. They loved it, every confrontation, from Sunday to Wednesday night when, out of national embarrassment, the National Guard had to be called in to replace them. I still have newspaper clippings from that week: cops smiling as they spray mace at a photographer, cops laughing as they beat and kick a group of fallen protesters. Yes, it was such a party that off-duty law enforcement and military personnel hurried downtown to get a piece of the action. An orgy, Chicago style.

Grant Park, Chicago, Illinois, August 28,1968 (UPI file photograph).

And why not admit it? We loved it, too. Screaming obscenities at the "pigs." Throwing rocks. Provoking them to acts of brutality. Mocking the patriarchal authority they represented. Cursing the leaders and the institutions they served so subserviently. And exposing, for all the world to see, the hypocrisy of the law and order crowd and the banality of the violence that was their last and only resort. No, there were no innocent bystanders on either side of the barricades in Chicago.

Sunday and Monday weren't enough. We all came back for more on Tuesday. I drove downtown to the Knickerbocker Hotel, where George McGovern was addressing the Nebraska delegation. One of the Nebraska delegates had promised me a pass to get into the convention. So I came to collect, waiting at the door of the caucus room while McGovern made his pitch. McGovern didn't make much of an impression at the Knickerbocker, and neither did I with my torn corduroy sports coat and McCarthy buttons. My clothing reeked of tear gas, thanks to the Chicago Police. Not exactly what the Knickerbocker had in mind for its clientele. Or McGovern, for that matter. He frowned at me as he walked out of the caucus room, hurrying off with his entourage to the next political event.

I had more luck than McGovern. I managed to get a pass, and so later that evening I drove across town to the south side of Chicago. I had to present my pass at each of the police barricades surrounding the amphitheater. Once inside I discovered that all the gallery seats in the balcony were taken. That was no problem as far as I was concerned, but the security guards had different ideas. They wouldn't allow me on the convention floor, and when I tried to watch from the first-floor exits I was told to take my seat.

"I don't have a seat," I said. "There aren't any more seats in the gallery."

"Then you'll have to keep moving," I was told.

So move I did, going from one exit to another until I was told to move on. Finally I got tired of musical chairs, so I called it a night and headed back to Evanston.

Then came Black Wednesday, the day the Democratic Party self-destructed. We didn't know it was Black Wednesday, of course. How could anyone have known what was going to happen on Michigan Avenue? By chance we decided to remain at the house in Evanston that night and watch the convention on television. We didn't want to miss Hubert Humphrey's nomination, the final act of betrayal. But as we watched, news coverage shifted to downtown Chicago, where hundreds of protesters had just been beaten by police. The young people were attempting to march to the Amphitheater when Mayor Daley's boys caught up with them at the corner of Michigan and Balboa, directly in front of the Hilton. For all the world to see. A beating to end all beatings. CBS anchorman Walter Cronkite was visibly shaken on the screen. He had seen police brutality in Selma and Birmingham, but nothing like this, he said. Cronkite's colleague, Eric Sevareid, agreed.

"Just about everything that needs saying has been said except one thing, that this is the most disgraceful night in the history of American political conventions," Sevareid concluded. "And I don't mean what happened in this hall but what happened in downtown Chicago."

So how could we stay away? Within minutes we were on our way downtown. When my VW refused to start, we simply called a taxi and took another twelve dollar ride to the riots. By the time we arrived downtown the protesters had regrouped in Grant Park, across from the Hilton. We joined them, chanting "Hey...Hey...LBJ. How many kids did you kill today?" as if Lyndon Johnson were hiding inside, afraid to come out. He wasn't, of course. He and his gang of patriarchs were at the Amphitheater voting, at that very moment, for Hubert Humphrey.

The mood that night was as poisoned as the air, still stinking of mace and tear gas. We taunted the police, and the police taunted us back, while spectators watched from the upper windows of the Hilton, waiting for the spark that would ignite the political powder keg below. If the spark came, downtown Chicago would go up in flames. Spontaneous combustion.

Suddenly the night turned surreal. We heard a low, rumbling sound over the shouting. It seemed to come from all directions at once. Confused, I ran into the street and saw a long line of jeeps and armored vehicles coming down Michigan Avenue. "The National Guard! They're bringing in the National Guard!" I shouted to no one in particular.

Talk about dislocation. Talk about unreality. The scene could have come out of a science fiction movie. Or a political thriller. State of siege politics, South America style. Dozens of military vehicles arriving. Hundreds of troops in combat gear running to take up positions along Michigan Avenue. The guardsmen carried rifles and what looked like ammunition belts. They used their vehicles as barricades. Some of the vehicles had barbed wire barriers fixed on their bumpers. "Prague West!" someone shouted, referring to the Russian invasion of Czechoslovakia one week earlier.

Time seemed to bend, to slow down to a kind of dream motion. Too much noise. Too many people. Thousands of angry people jammed together in one tiny corner of time and space. We couldn't move. All we could do was sit down on the grass and try to remain calm. Mary Travers and Peter Yarrow appeared and started the crowd singing. Singing helped ease the tension.

So, too, did listening to the speeches of the celebrities who came over from the Hilton. We listened to Norman Mailer, John Kenneth Galbraith, and Julian Bond. And we listened to Gore Vidal, who earlier that evening had become something of a folk hero by referring to William F. Buckley, Jr. as a "crypto-Nazi" live on national television. Vidal and Buckley were providing commentary for ABC's convention coverage when they disagreed over the causes of the violence erupting both on the floor of the convention and outside in the streets. Vidal's comment prompted Buckley to lunge forward and say, "I'll punch you in the goddamn face." After which the moderator, Howard K. Smith, concluded: "This exchange has shed more heat than light." Yes, indeed. Howard might not have known it then, but Vidal versus Buckley was the perfect political allegory for that entire week in Chicago.

Later, after the convention had ended for the night, we heard that some of the McCarthy delegates were on their way to join us. They had formed a candlelight procession and were walking to the Hilton. As it turned out, they walked only part of the way. Even so, it took them until three a.m. to walk those last few blocks. We cheered when we saw the rows of glowing candles coming up Michigan Avenue and heard the delegates singing, "We Shall Overcome."

We stayed in Grant Park all that night. And we came back the next day, after another attempted march to the Amphitheater and another confrontation, this time with the National Guard. Thursday night's crowd was smaller, though. By this time the violence had taken its toll: too many arrested, too many injured. But those of us who remained came back for one final all-night vigil. We listened to Ralph Abernathy and Allen Ginsberg and then McCarthy himself tell us that the struggle would not end in Chicago but would continue.

"I am happy to address the government in exile," McCarthy said. He urged his followers to support candidates for the U.S. Senate who opposed the war in Vietnam. "We have tested the process and found its weaknesses," he said. "We'll make this party in 1972 quite different from what we found in Chicago."

Pula, Yugoslavia. August 1, 1972

Since the day I'd run afoul of Tito and his goons, when I came a missed translation away from being arrested and deported, I'd begun to notice the presence of Yugoslav soldiers pretty much everywhere I went. I began to feel like Daniel Cohn-Bendit must have felt right before the French arrested and deported him back to Germany for his role in the '68 Paris Barricades. I saw the soldiers waiting at bus stops and standing on street corners, outside restaurants, sometimes inside restaurants, staking out the exits. I saw them in the park across the street from our room, apparently watching us through the open window, which had provided the stage for my supposed terrorist transgression. Every morning they were waiting with pressed brown uniforms and automatic weapons when we went to the bakery next door for breakfast, and every evening they were waiting outside our apartment when we returned to our room from a night of partying along the waterfront. A couple of times one of them pinched Chantal's ass as we walked by, and when she let loose with an obscenity or two, "*Ta gueule!*" or "*Va te faire fautre!*" the sexist pig would glare at me, daring me to say or do anything by way of response.

I held my tongue, not wanting to end up in one of Tito's dungeons because of a little ass pinching.

What freaked me out even more was that for the past week or so I'd been catching glimpses of a huge white car trailing me from a distance. The car looked to me like an American Cadillac with darkened windows. Whenever I tried to approach, the mysterious car disappeared quickly around a corner, lost in a maze of twisting cobblestone streets. Was it real, or was it only a hallucination, a sure sign of paranoia on my part? I never knew for certain because I could never catch up with the white beast, which I dubbed Moby Cadillac and which, like Ahab's white whale, taunted me mercilessly. If the car was real and not imaginary, then what did its presence signify? Was the American Embassy in Belgrade after me as well as Tito and his henchmen? Had I become an international revolutionary to be hunted down in the streets of Pula like a common criminal?

Today, leaving Veruda Beach, we were followed to the bus stop by another brown-suited soldier, this one so young he looked like a teenager, dwarfed by the automatic weapon he carried on his back. When the bus stopped, he climbed on board and sat up front by the driver but glanced back over his shoulder from time to time, as though keeping an eye on all the passengers on board, or maybe just us, who knew for sure. Freaking out, I nudged Chantal as we approached Pula and pulled the cord to get off. "*Pourquoi?*" she asked, but followed me down off the bus. "*Que fais-tu?*"

The young soldier glanced back at us just as we stepped off. It was too late for him to react. We watched his face, plastered against the window, fade into the distance as the bus roared off toward the center of Pula.

Now that we were alone, I motioned for Chantal to follow me. We hiked in silence across a small park, coming finally to the ruins of one of Pula's two Roman theaters, this one dating from the first century A.D. Measuring about 100 meters in diameter, the theater and its circular stone benches had been dug out of the side of a hill. The benches were mostly intact, but nothing remained of its proscenium except for scattered slices of marble columns that seemed tossed like dice by the huge hands of Roman gods. We sat facing each other on adjacent marble fragments. Chantal wanted to know what the hell was going on. She waited impatiently for my explanation.

"I think we're under surveillance. Maybe I'm paranoid, but I think that young soldier on the bus was following us."

Chantal looked at me as though I had completely lost my mind. "*Bien sûr. Tu es le paranoïaque?*"

With that, we both broke out laughing. We couldn't stop laughing, sitting there among the marble ruins of a Roman theater where two thousand years earlier Roman plays by Terence, Plautus, Seneca, and Andronicus, and Greek plays by Euripedes, Sophocles, Aeschylus, and Aristophanes were performed in the original Latin and Greek. It was a humbling experience to sit there surrounded by the ghosts of antiquity and to know that some of the greatest drama produced by Western Civilization had been performed on this very spot two millennia before. In the long sweep of history both individuals and nations seemed insignificant. Of what consequence were we, were our two countries, compared to the magnificence of Greece and Rome?

The laughter helped. I felt much better afterward, less paranoid and more able to deal with whatever lay ahead, Tito's goons or Moby Cadillac.

Taking our time, we walked back across the park and followed the main road into Pula, stopping for a bite to eat at a small café on the central plaza. Maybe it was my frame of mind, but I didn't notice a single soldier the entire time. It turned out to be a much longer walk than we imagined. By the time we reached our room we were hot and exhausted, so we stripped off our clothes and fell into bed, too tired for conversation.

M aili Losinj. August 4, 1972

Today we took an excursion boat to the island of Mali Losinj, about 70 kilometers south of Pula, heading toward Albania and Greece. The boat began boarding at nine a.m., which turned out to be a problem because I needed two or three cups of coffee to wake up in the morning. We made it just as the ship was about to leave, the last two people to board. From what I could tell, most of the other passengers were German. They gathered below on the lower deck, next to the bar, where they started drinking and smoking at that early hour of the morning. So we found seats on the upper deck, where we could avoid the Germans and enjoy the fresh air and sunshine.

Unlike the afternoon light, which took on a golden shade of amber as the day progressed, the early morning light was invariably a brilliant white, whitewashing the rocky coast of Istria, *une étude en noir et blanc*, as our boat chugged out to sea and the skyline of Pula disappeared around the curve of the peninsula. Our course along the coastline took us past one whitewashed rocky island after another, most of them appearing sparsely inhabited, if inhabited at all. How many Greek and Roman sailors, like Odysseus and Aeneas, had been lost at sea while exploring this coast? Getting lost would be easy here, since all the small islands looked about the same: hot, dry, parched to the color of sun-bleached bone. So desolate that you expected to see buzzards flying overhead, looking for carrion.

That changed when, two hours later, we approached Mali Losinj, an island much larger than the others we'd seen, with hills pockmarked by fig and palm trees and with rows of stone and stucco houses spilling down a steep incline to the water's edge. Our boat chugged through a narrow strait into a V-shaped port with docks and piers along each arm of the V and a small park at the tip. We were both eager to get off the boat and stretch our legs, find something to eat and settle our stomachs.

Taking our time, since we had four hours to kill until our boat left for the return trip to Pula, we stopped at a café for a light lunch, split a bottle of mineral water, and then explored the shops along the port, finding little of interest. Next, we hiked up the hill overlooking the port, along narrow cobblestone streets and rows of simple stone houses that reminded me of Greece. Everything bleached white by the midday sun. By this time we were hot, thirsty, and tired, so we made our way back down to the park where we bought another bottle of water from a vendor and found a bench in the shade of a massive palm tree. We still had an hour before departure.

We sat in silence for a few minutes, watching tourists strolling along the quay and boats gliding across the water out in the bay. Chantal was in one of her reflective moods, I could tell by the way she looked at me. Finally I worked up the courage, or maybe the honesty, to say what I had wanted to say for a very long time...to bring up the subject we had forbidden ourselves to talk or think about: the future.

"*Chantal*...what will happen to us at the end of the month?"

"*Que veux-tu dire?*" she asked, even though she knew perfectly well what I meant.

"I could stay in Strasbourg..."

"*Mais...comment?*"

"I could get a job, maybe teach English in some language school or give private lessons. Something like that."

Silence.

I tried again. "Or...you could come live with me."

"*Je ne peux pas parler l'anglais.*"

"You could find something...you could learn to speak English."

She shook her head. "*Non, pas possible....*"

I knew what she meant. She wanted a career, a meaningful job, a profession that meant something to her. Whatever the two of us had just wasn't enough. Not after her marriage and divorce.

When the time arrived, we left the shade of our palm tree and headed back to the boat. This time we skipped the upper deck and went down below, out of the sun, where we found the same group of loudmouth Germans, most of them men, gathered at the bar as before. Apparently they'd been drinking all day, on and off the boat. That morning they had seemed jovial and festive, anticipating the day's events, but drinking all day had turned them into an unsightly bunch of sloppy drunks, sour and depressed and mean-spirited.

The women sat off to the side, banished to a long table, where they sipped glasses of wine or mixed drinks and talked among themselves, looking bored and unhappy.

I found a seat far away from the bar and then went to buy two beers. Halfway through the cold beer I started to feel better, less sun-struck and irritable, until just as we pulled away from the dock to begin the return trip to Pula, one of the drunks pulled a trumpet out of his backpack and started playing off-key versions of German drinking songs, while his cohorts splashed their beers in the air and belted out the lyrics: "Bier her, bier her, oder ich fall um, juchhe! Bier her, bier her, oder ich full um!" They got drunker and sloppier as the voyage progressed, one of them falling asleep with his head resting on the bar. I reached the limit of my patience when the trumpeter began playing a crude version of "Auld Lang Syne."

The drunks, getting sentimental now, began to hug and slap each other on the back. It was too much to bear.

"*Assez!*" I said, loud enough for everyone to hear, even the drunks.

We left the table and stepped outside, back to peace and quiet and a magnificent view of the setting sun.

What a depressing vision of middle age, I remarked to Chantal. Was it inevitable that all of us would fall victim to failed marriages and broken lives and be reduced to old, fat, sloppy drunks making a public spectacle of ourselves? I wanted desperately to believe otherwise, but most middle-aged people I encountered seemed so miserable, so bereft of joy and happiness.

Huddled on the upper deck we watched the bright red disc of the sun disappear slowly into the Adriatic, leaving a pink smudge on the western horizon, a stain on paradise.

That sunset turned out to be an omen because, unknown to us, our paradise was about to come to a crashing end.

Pula, Yugoslavia. August 11, 1972

This morning we were strolling down the avenue past the coliseum on our way to a food market to buy snacks for the beach when I heard someone shout out behind me "James Wilson." I froze instantly, as though I had been shot in the back, ambushed by a sniper. Who knew my name here? I stumbled forward a step or two, rattled and confused, feeling trapped. More than anything else I felt discovered, exposed. Pursued by Tito and his goons or the Chicago Police, by bounty hunters who had tracked me down all the way to Pula, the far ends of the earth. My refuge, my hidden life, all vanished instantly as I stood there frozen. Chantal looked back over her shoulder, as confused as I was. She moved away from me, as though I were a criminal about to be impounded and escorted away. Guilt by association.

Then I heard a familiar laugh, a wicked cackle that I recognized instantly, and turned to see an old friend from home in what was then and still is the strangest, most unbelievable coincidence in my life. Not just an old friend, but someone who I had known and lived with for years, one of my very best friends. It was none other than Joe, a freak and fellow counterculture traveler, and his equally hip wife Faye. They looked tan and reasonably straight, with yellow granny shades and backpacks. I must have looked like I was having a stroke, mouth hanging open, unable to speak for a long moment. How?

The yacht on which Joe and Faye arrived in Pula, Yugoslavia, 1972 (courtesy of Faye Agustine).

So instead of me explaining this unlikely coincidence, I'll let Joe tell the story as he told it to those at our table and anyone else who would listen later that evening at our café:

"No way, man. No fucking way I expected to run into James in a remote place like Yugoslavia. He's a friend from the university back home, but I hadn't seen him for weeks and I had no idea he was in living in Pula with a French chick. Faye and I were sailing up the coast on our way to Trieste and Venice on this big fucking yacht—a sixty-footer owned by Andy here, our filthy rich English friend, whose family keeps the yacht and its crew docked in Athens, if you can dig it. We'd spent the last month stoned out of our minds, swimming and snorkeling in the Adriatic, and seriously depleting our stash of drugs. Every few days we put in at a port along the coast in order to replenish our supplies. That's the reason we ended up in Pula.

"So Faye and I had just gone to a drug store in the city center and were walking back to the waterfront when, out of the blue, I spotted James up ahead. At first I didn't know if I could believe my eyes. Was it really James, or was I flashing again? I'd been seeing lots of weird stuff, especially out on the sea where there's nothing to fucking see except the water and what's in your head. 'Check it out,' I said to Faye, pointing to the dude up ahead who looked like James. 'I think that's James Wilson.'

"Faye shot me one of her disapproving looks and said, 'You're tripping. Knock off the drugs.'

"'Oh yeah, well let's find out.' So I shouted: 'James Wilson!'

"Sure enough, he stopped dead in his tracks. I mean he froze, like he'd just been smoked out, like he'd been hiding incognito in Yugoslavia or Albania or wherever and now he'd been spotted, caught red-handed in broad daylight. At first I thought the crazy fucker might run the other way, not wanting to be recognized. Instead, he turned and looked over his shoulder, then said, 'Holy shit! What are you doing here?' The French chick looked confused, like she didn't have a clue about what was happening.

"'Man, what are *you* doing here?'

"He explained that he and the French chick, whose name was Chantal, were vacationing in Pula for the summer. 'Groovy, man,' I said, eying Chantal. She was a hot number, with long dark hair and a nice ass, but kind of standoffish and not very friendly, the French way.

"'So what are you doing here?' James asked again.

"'Oh yeah, well, we just got off a boat.' I started to point over to the harbor where our friend's yacht was moored until Faye stepped in and completed my story, telling them about our English friend and his family yacht and how we were in Pula for only one day, leaving tomorrow, all the details that I'd left out, not on purpose, just the way my mind works, a brief lapse every now and again, no big deal. I don't like to get bogged down in details. I'm more of a big picture kind of guy.

"James explained the situation to Chantal, who looked less confused but just as unfriendly. Actually, they both looked a little pissed off at being discovered, a little resentful maybe. Like we'd intruded on their Summer of Love or something.

"'Far out,' I said, trying to dispel the awkwardness. Then I had an idea. Trying to use what little French I'd learned at the university, I said to Chantal, 'Hey...*voulez vous...manger*...lunch?'

"She turned to James. 'Manger?'

"James nodded. 'Si.'

"Chantal turned back to me. 'Si.'

"'I could eat,' Faye said. "First, though, let's give you a tour of the yacht. Wait until you see this rig. It's incredible.'

"So they followed us to the dock, where the yacht was anchored. Faye explained that it slept nine people, including the four members of the crew. One of the crew, Danny, was sitting on the deck reading when we came aboard. He flashed us a peace sign, then ignored us as we took James and Chantal down into the cabin, all dark polished wood and shiny brass, like a fancy hotel room or a real cool bachelor pad, with plush seats and beds and lots of cool nautical stuff. Kitchen, bedrooms, bathrooms, it had everything you needed to feel at home. You could even sail around the world if you wanted to, as long as you had enough drugs to last you however long it took.

"'You should see it with the sails up, man,' I said. 'It's a real trip... fucking beautiful.'

"'Wow,' was all James could say.

"While Faye showed them the bedrooms, I rolled a number and passed it around. 'Here's to my man, McGovern,' I said. 'He's going to legalize pot.' Then I rolled another number. By the time we finished that one we were all hungry, so we went down the harbor to a sidewalk restaurant and ordered food and a bottle of wine, some local Yugoslav white wine that tasted like piss mixed with sugar. Bummer. But it was cheap, so we ordered another bottle, which I mostly drank by myself. Turned out that James and the French chick, whose name I could no longer remember, were going to the beach that afternoon, while we had to finish shopping for supplies. So we decided to meet for dinner that evening at another outdoor cafe that had music and better wine, according to James, who didn't know shit about wine since he didn't drink it, so go figure.

"Before we split, I asked James if what's her name really didn't speak English or if she was just being unfriendly, like the French.

"'No, she doesn't speak English, but she can sing a couple of Beatles' songs when she's drunk. Or so she claims.'

"'I can dig it. I like the Beatles when I'm drunk.'

"After they left, I was feeling a little woozy, so I let Faye do the shopping while I went back to the yacht and crashed. Once I hit the mattress I was out like a light. It was like falling over a cliff into a deep sleep. The next thing I remember was Faye shaking me awake, hollering for me to open my eyes. Behind her Danny was giving her advice on what to do next: try mouth to mouth, slap the motherfucker, that sort of thing. 'What happened? Where am I? What are you doing?' I asked, swatting her away. For a moment I thought she was trying to strangle me. I thought they wanted to kill me so they could have the drugs all to themselves, the bastards!

"'I thought you were dead. You freaked me out,' Faye said.

"'Dead? I don't think so.' I looked around. 'Must be the weed. Or that cheap white wine.'

"'You didn't take any other drugs, did you?'

"'Not yet.'

"'Well, don't! You're starting to lose it.'

"Turns out, I'd slept all afternoon. I barely had time to wash my face and put on a clean shirt before we left for dinner. Maybe I should cut down on the drugs, maybe I was losing it, like Faye said. I'd have to think about that one tomorrow.

"Anyway, when I was awake, we rounded up Andy and the four of you blokes on crew and headed down to the waterfront."

So went Joe's tale of the strangest day of my life and possibly of his, although given his affinity for psychedelic substances, who knows?

That said, I'll take over for Joe now, since I was there and can attest to their stately arrival, Joe, Faye, Andy, and their crew. What a sight it was, a blur of long hair, baggy shorts, ripped tee-shirts and flip-flops, punctuated by loud voices cursing and the screech of chairs being pushed out of the way. Everybody gawked at them when they burst onto the patio, six groovy guys and one hippie chick, all Anglo-Americans with long unkempt hair and attitudes to match.

Or, as Joe remarked to me later in private, boasting a bit, they ran loud and rowdy and obnoxious, especially the crew. A bunch of soccer hooligans from Manchester, they drank and fought at every possible opportunity. "They love to fight," Joe said. "And man, if you dare insult Manchester United, they will stomp your ass and then piss on your face. Mean fuckers."

According to Joe, on the voyage up the coast it was always a miracle when they managed to get out of a port without starting a fight.

"There...I see the wankers!" Danny yelled, pointing to the table in back where Chantal and I were seated. Chantal seemed to shrink back, as though having second thoughts about being seen with these crazy Anglos.

"Hey, man, why so far away from the action?" Joe asked.

I motioned toward the table. "We took the biggest table. We can all fit."

"Oh, yeah, good thinking," he said.

Andy went directly to the bar and ordered drinks for everyone. He returned with bottles of wine and liters of beer, all carried by an obliging waitress, who looked old and tired and in no mood for Andy and his friends. She set the bottles down carefully, one at a time, while keeping a suspicious eye on Andy.

"Drink up, lads and lasses, but watch what you say," Andy said. "Remember what happened in Dubrovnik. We were nearly arrested."

"Arrested?" I asked.

"Yeah, we poured beer on this ass-hole," Danny explained. "He heard us talking about his girlfriend...we were wondering if she liked oral sex. He took exception to how Patch here was behaving."

Patch, the oldest and meanest of the crew, flicked his tongue in and out, as if he were performing cunnilingus on his glass of beer. "I could tell the wench liked tongue by the way she smiled at me. That's why the bloke got pissed...because she was more interested in me than in him. I could have showed her a right proper time."

"Absolutely," Andy said. "That's why we had to pour beer on him, but you didn't have to slap him around, Patch old boy."

"I only slapped him once. Maybe twice."

"Commie motherfuckers!" Danny said. "We'll kick their ass in the Olympics week after next."

Joe slapped his forehead. "Far out, man, I forgot the Summer Olympics this month. Munich, right?"

"That's right, Germany. We'll kick their ass, too."

Faye rolled her eyes, then smiled and motioned to Chantal, the two of them taking turns pouring themselves tall glasses of wine, trying to pretend they didn't know the obnoxious males sitting at their table. Amused, all I could do was sit back, drink glasses of beer, and watch the party unfold. I'd known Joe for many years, and I knew he was capable of just about anything, and as for the crew, I couldn't imagine anyone ever being able to control their behavior. But I'll give them credit, they kept the peace, managing to make it through the dinner without getting thrown out or even insulting anyone really, except the waitress who was way too slow to keep up with our drink orders and deserved all the insults, though maybe not the slap on the ass. Danny knocked over a bottle of wine while lighting a cigarette, and Patch called him a dumb motherfucker, but other than that one tiny incident, we were perfect gentlemen all night long, or at least until Chantal and I left about midnight.

When we got up to go, Danny and the boys gave us a hard time, called us wussies and party poopers. Someone made the crack that before Chantal could leave, she would have to be civil for one goddamn moment and say something, anything in English. So Chantal stood up unsteadily, grabbed the table for balance, and sang in a Frenchified English accent:

"Yesterday, all my troubles seemed so far away...now it looks as though they're here to stay, oh yesterday...."

Everybody applauded, even Danny and Patch.

"See, she does speak English," Joe said.

"Non, Je ne parle pas anglais," Chantal said. "Je parle Beatles."

"Yeah, me too, especially the Walrus song," Joe said. Then he grabbed my shoulder and said, "Adios, bro. See you back in the States!"

Pula, Yugoslavia. August 20, 1972

Our summer had turned a corner. The wind had gone out of our sails. Suddenly we found ourselves unmoored, drifting toward September without a plan and without direction. It was as though we awoke one morning to find the outside world encroaching upon our lotus land, our summer of forgetfulness, as Chantal predicted it would. Always a fatalist, she believed it was impossible to run away from the past, since in essence we are the past, having been shaped by everything we have experienced, the good as well as the bad. But what about the future, I always asked. Can't we plan a future that's separate from, or at least different from the past? Can't we make a clean break?

Seeing Joe and Faye had reminded me of all I'd hoped to leave behind by coming to Europe. They brought more bad news from home: news about the unending war and the increasingly nasty presidential campaign. "They won't give peace a chance," Joni Mitchell sang, "that was just a dream some of us had." Nothing much had changed since Mitchell recorded "California" in 1970. Nixon was still bombing North Vietnam, American soldiers and Vietnamese civilians were still being slaughtered in South Vietnam. To make matters worse, the McGovern campaign had already begun to unravel after his running mate, Sen. Thomas Eagleton, had been forced to withdraw from the ticket when it became known that he had a history of being treated for mental disorders. It looked increasingly likely that in November Nixon would be re-elected for four more bloody years.

Almost against my will, I found myself drawn back into the fray. I wanted to vote for a peace candidate who would end the war, I wanted to vote against Nixon and Kissinger and all the felons (we found out later) who ran the Watergate operation. Likewise, there were things I'd left undone back home: people, relationships, graduate school. Before moving on I needed to finish graduate school. Then I could walk away and launch myself into an unknown future in France or wherever, with or without Chantal. I needed closure before I could embrace a future.

Even our daily trips to Veruda Beach were qualitatively different than before. The angle of the sun had decreased over the course of the summer, so that the light now had a fleeting quality, a pale yellow glow that seemed increasingly feeble, incapable of producing the warmth of July or early August. Accordingly, the crowds had thinned out as the tourists headed back home to Germany or England or wherever their place of origin, leaving those of us who remained behind with an end-of-the-season malaise. Every day fewer stragglers showed up on the beach with towels and sunscreen and the other accoutrements of summer. It was time for us to go, but go where?

Sitting in our room this morning, looking out on the nearly deserted harbor, I told Chantal that I was thinking about going home at the end of the month. Just to take care of unfinished business.

She nodded. *"Je sais...quand tu étais avec tes amis, j'ai vu."*

"Would you come with me?" I knew she wouldn't because she was scheduled to start teaching next month, but I had to ask anyway. I had to try.

"C'est impossible."

"Could you come to visit me during the year?"

She thought for a long moment before saying she could probably come during Christmas break. That was good enough.

By the time we left for the beach we'd formulated a plan. I would finally get serious about my studies and finish graduate school while Chantal taught school in Strasbourg during the coming year. She would come to the States and spend two weeks with me during Christmas. Then I would return to Strasbourg in June, so the two of us could go to Greece for the rest of the summer, after which we would see what happened. I might remain in Strasbourg permanently, or I might not, depending on how we felt. No promises, only a decision to wait and see how we felt at the end of the following summer. It seemed like a sensible plan. Workable. A plan we both could live with.

Still, I felt conflicted, drawn back to the States but also wanting to stay with Chantal. On the way back from the beach that afternoon we stopped in the city center, where there were pay phones available on the plaza. I needed to call Air France, change my open-ended ticket and make a return reservation. When I approached the phone banks, though, I had a moment of doubt. We sat on one of the benches and watched people crisscross the paved plaza, old women dressed all in black pulling two-wheeled shopping carts behind them, old men with gray beards playing chess on the plaza tables, and screaming children kicking a soccer ball against a concrete wall. Finally, after several minutes of silence, I got up, walked to the nearest phone, and made the call, reserving a seat August 26 on the Air France flight from Paris to Chicago. Just like that it was done, over. The summer had a definite end point, a formal conclusion, a termination. What had seemed infinite now seemed merely finite. I felt as though I had just learned the date of my own death.

Chantal took my hand, and together we walked in silence across the plaza and down the street to our room.

Part 2 / In Transit

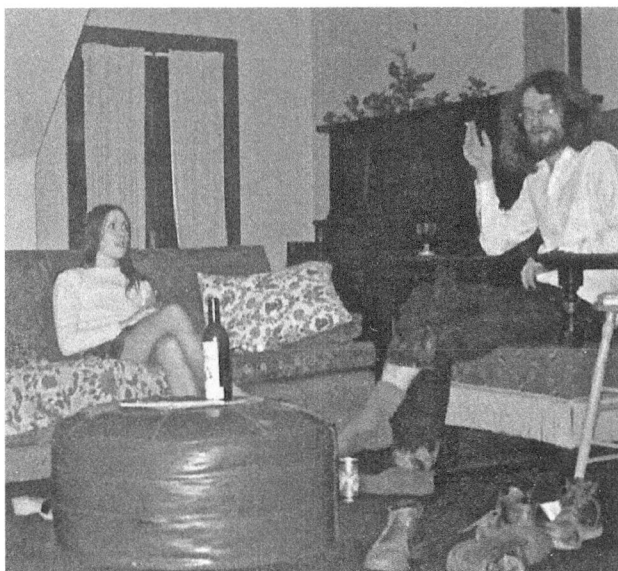

Chantal and Ross at 1631 F Street, Lincoln, Nebraska, 1973 (author's collection).

S trasbourg, France. August 23, 1972

Our train pulled into the Strasbourg station well after ten p.m. We were completely exhausted from a long day of traveling, a day in which we had retraced our journey at the end of June, which now seemed light-years away. First the bus ride from Pula to Trieste (this time, instead of detaining me, the Yugoslav border patrol took one look at my passport and expedited my departure, glad to get rid of me), followed by the train from Trieste to

Milan, and finally the long train ride from Milan to Strasbourg. We had just enough energy left to collect our bags and walk the ten or so blocks to Chantal's new apartment, now empty and available for her to occupy. Before we left, she'd managed to get a key to the apartment and to move a few of her belongings. This meant we didn't have to disturb her parents and sisters, who would be sound asleep at this hour. Even better, it meant that we would have a place of our own for our last few days together in Strasbourg.

Her apartment was on the second floor of a yellow stone building, above a row of small shops, all closed down tight for the night. We carried our bags up the stairs, opened the door, and looked in on an empty one-room apartment that, at first glance, did not look all that inviting. But there was a studio kitchen with a sink and hotplate, a small bathroom, and a bed in the center of the room, all the necessities. We didn't bother to unpack or do anything with the apartment. Instead, we put sheets on the bed, grabbed a blanket, and went to sleep without saying a word. All things considered, it was a depressing homecoming. Talking about it would have made it worse.

We awoke to bright sunshine streaming through the front window and a much more cheerful day. From the double window, we looked out over the broad avenue to the green hills just beyond the city, where the Rhine River cut through the Vosges. Since we didn't have any food in the apartment, we went out for coffee and croissants at the nearest bakery, after which Chantal wanted to do some shopping for her apartment. I tagged along for a while, helping her pick out cooking utensils, bedding supplies, and the like, until I reached my limit of domesticity. Chantal understood.

"*Va...fais que tu veux. Ca m'occupe,*" she said, pointing to the shelves of household items surrounding us.

So after making arrangements to meet her later that afternoon at her apartment, I took off to find a copy of the *Herald Tribune*. Then I walked to the river *Ill* and followed it to the historic city center. My favorite spot in Strasbourg was on the *Barrage Vauban*, just across the river from the *Grande Ile*. From the benches there I had a spectacular view of the island and all three spans of the medieval stone bridge known as the *Ponts Couverts*. To the right Strasbourg's most famous structure, the Gothic Cathedral of Our Lady, towered over the narrow medieval streets. When catching the sun just right, the red sandstone cathedral resembled a giant flame shooting into the sky.

Sitting there, I skimmed the front-page articles in the *Tribune*, not finding any political news of interest. The Republicans were convening in Miami to re-nominate Richard Nixon as their presidential candidate, no surprise there. I was more interested in an article about the ongoing chess match between American Bobby Fischer and Boris Spassky of the U.S.S.R. The match, held in Reykjavik, Iceland, featured all the tensions and nuances of the Cold War as the irascible but brilliant Fischer continued to dominate the current world champion. In fact, Fischer was on the verge of winning the match and becoming the 11th (and first American) world chess champion.

I'd just opened the newspaper, intending to read the inside pages, when I heard footsteps and a male voice.

"Hey, man, what's happening. Are you American?"

I looked up at a short, dark-haired man wearing a navy blazer and slacks, no tie. He looked to be in his thirties, maybe early forties.

"Guilty as charged. Who wants to know?"

He laughed. "Name's Richard. I'm from New Jersey. I saw you reading the *Tribune* and thought you might be American. Mind if I sit down?"

He helped himself before I could answer. "I've lived here for five years now, ever since I married a French woman. I love France, but sometimes I miss hearing English. Not many people in Strasbourg speak English. In Paris, yes, but not in Strasbourg. Here everything's French or German."

"Really? As a matter of fact I happen to be living with a French woman at the moment. We're not married, but who knows."

"No shit! Well, I highly recommend marriage. Especially if you're going to live in France, where marriage is less rigid, if you follow what I'm saying. It's not the same as it is back in the states where you're expected to be faithful and monogamous till death do you part. Everybody here fools around, gets a little on the side, it's expected. No one makes a big deal about it. And hey, don't you love French women? They're totally uninhibited. The sex is great!"

I agreed. "So what do you do? How do you make a living in Strasbourg?" I was interested because, though I'd been trying all summer, I just couldn't imagine a future life for me in Strasbourg. I couldn't see myself sitting around all day waiting for Chantal to get off work, or teaching English part-time at some nondescript language institute. I needed a sense of professionalism, a *métier* as Chantal would say. Maybe it was a failure of imagination on my part, but I was coming around to Chantal's point of view.

He handed me a business card with his name and the words, "Sports Car Enthusiast," printed on blue parchment paper. "Yeah, my wife works for the European Parliament, so I don't have to worry about making a living. I mostly dabble in sports cars. At the moment I have a sweet little Mercedes Coupe. Before that it was an Alfa Romeo. The Germans, French, and Italians make the best sports cars in the world. Someday I'd like to open my own automobile franchise and specialize in sports cars, but it's not easy to do in France. There's lots of red tape, especially for an American citizen, even if he's married to a French woman. We'll see, I'm still working on it."

"Hey—the red tape can't be any worse than Jersey."

He laughed. "You'd be surprised. So anyway, what's up with your French woman? What's the story?"

I told him about Chantal, that I'd decided to return to the States to finish graduate school and take care of unfinished business and then come back to Strasbourg in June, maybe permanently, if I could figure out something to do with myself, a job or some appointment at the American embassy or the American library.

"No way, man. You're going to leave for a year and expect Chantal to be faithful, to be waiting for you when you come back? The French don't think like that. If you're gone, you're gone. The French don't believe that gods–or lovers–manifest themselves by their absence. They want a warm body in their bed. Not like back in the States, where chicks want love and romance and happily ever after. The French see through all that bullshit, they get down to the real nitty gritty."

"Sex, you mean."

"Bingo!"

I laughed.

"Or maybe I'm just a sex addict. My wife says I'm a sex addict and that's why I love living in France. I think she's joking, but maybe not."

I laughed. "I'll drink to that."

"Yeah? You have time for a beer? It's on me, my friend."

"Why not," I said, since I had lots of time to kill before I was supposed to meet Chantal.

So we crossed the bridge into the historic district, where we found an empty table at an outdoor café just down the street and around the corner from the cathedral. He told me more about his wife, who worked as an interpreter for the European Parliament and who was fluent in six languages, which was (he pointed out) at least four more than we were fluent in. He said he didn't miss New Jersey or living in the States, except for the language. As much as he loved spoken French, he missed having a conversation in English with friends who understood where he was coming from and his Jersey street rap. We parted after a couple of beers by shaking hands and promising to get together if and when I returned to Strasbourg the following Spring.

Paris, France. August 26, 1972

I left Paris on the day the 1972 Olympics opened in Munich. I was tired, cranky, and in no mood for the perky young woman sitting next to me on the plane. I'd seen her in the waiting room at Orly, bouncing around in her seat and singing softly to herself, oblivious to the stares of those sitting around her. Her behavior, though odd, was no crazier than her felt hat, not a sexy fedora, but a squashed green pork pie hat that an elderly man might have worn but not an attractive young blonde who couldn't have been more than twenty years old. As we boarded the plane I thanked my lucky stars that the chances were remote that my seat would be anywhere near hers. Well, guess what? She was waiting for me when I stumbled down the aisle to my seat and stowed my gear in the overhead compartment.

"I switched seats with you. I didn't think you'd mind," she said, sitting in my window seat.

I barely had enough time to sit down in my–that is, her–seat before she let out a whoop and pumped her fist in the air three times. "Isn't it great to be going home!"

"I guess," I said, thinking she must be an American student studying abroad. Maybe she'd been gone for the year and that's why she was so excited to be going home to her friends and family.

"The good ole U–S–of–A!" she squealed.

"So how long have you been gone...the summer, or the whole year?"

"Since yesterday," she said, and pumped her fist in the air a couple more times. She still hadn't removed her pork pie hat, which was pulled down over a wisp of blond hair.

"Excuse me?"

"See, there was a mix-up," she began, and while we prepared for take-off, I listened to her incredible story. It seems the day before she had flown from Chicago to Paris, planning to meet up with some friends who were renting an apartment on the Left Bank, but when she got to Paris she discovered they'd skipped town and left no forwarding address. So what did she do? She walked around Paris yesterday afternoon and evening, checked into a youth hostel for one night, and changed her ticket for this morning's flight back to Chicago. And here she was, sitting next to me in my window seat, now telling me about all the sites she'd seen on her afternoon walk: Notre Dame, the Seine, the Louvre, the Champs Elysée, and the ever popular Eiffel Tower. "I saw everything I wanted to see and more," she bragged.

"Really? Did you like Paris?"

She shrugged. "It's okay, I guess, but it's no Chicago!" She whooped again and pumped her fist. I could understand why her friends would want to ditch her, who wouldn't? By this time I was looking around for an empty seat, but the Air France flight was completely full, which meant I was stuck for the duration of the ten-hour flight. Lucky me.

"You're from Chicago? And you like it?"

"What's wrong with Chicago?" she snapped back at me.

I told her what was wrong with Chicago, beginning with Mayor Daley and the Chicago Police, and ending with my experience at the 1968 Democratic National Convention. Nice place if you want to get tear-gassed, beaten, and brutalized, I said, unfairly.

Now she was furious. "So that was you!" She said it as if I had been the only demonstrator at the convention, as if it had been personal, me versus Chicago. "Well, let me tell you something, buster. You and the other radicals might not like him, but Mayor Daley is a great man and a great mayor. He keeps the city running like clockwork: the garbage gets picked up, the snow gets removed from the streets, and the buses run on time. Chicago's the greatest city in the world, and that includes Paris. Who needs the French, anyway? They can keep their Eiffel Tower. Gimme Chicago any day."

I checked again for an empty seat somewhere in the rear of the plane, far away from Miss Chicago.

Suddenly she burst out in song: "Chicago! Chicago! My kind of town!"

Fortunately one of the flight attendants came to my rescue, telling us to fasten our seatbelts and prepare for take-off and, by implication, to shut up.

As soon as we were in the air and had reached our cruising altitude, the young woman perked up. "Oh well, let's make up and be friends. I'm Ellie."

Then she buzzed the attendant and asked for a Coke, which she downed in a few big gulps. Ten minutes later she excused herself to go pee. Then she ordered another Coke, which she drank down just as quickly and then climbed over me again to go pee. This went on for about an hour—Coke, pee, Coke, pee—with me thinking all the while that the last thing Ellie needed was more caffeinated drinks loaded with sugar.

Eventually the sugar high passed and left her slumped over and limp, her head bobbing against my shoulder. Her hat, squished between the two of us, rubbed against my bare skin and itched like hell. Now what was I supposed to do, I remember thinking, as I tried to move sideways, away from the slumping young woman who was now snoring and drooling on my shoulder. I moved again, this time a bit too far, which allowed her head to plop down in my lap, her hat falling between my legs and landing on my foot. Without her hat she looked very young and very pretty, I couldn't help but notice. It was the first kind thought I'd had about Ellie, but it didn't last very long.

"Hey!" She jerked her head up out of my lap, awake now. "Are you getting fresh with me? Are you trying to take advantage of me?"

The attendant rushed over to calm the situation. "Is there a problem here?"

"You bet there is, he's getting fresh with me. I woke up with my face in his lap. His crotch!"

"That's because you fell asleep," I protested, mostly to the flight attendant, who looked at us like we were insane, a couple of loonies. Just like that my warm feeling toward Ellie was gone with the wind.

"Well, please keep it down," the attendant said, frowned, and walked away.

"Here." I reached down and picked up Ellie's hat. "Let's make up and be friends. I'm James."

That seemed to satisfy her, at least temporarily. I tried to defuse the situation by keeping busy, first reading the in-flight magazine and then writing in my journal, which I had woefully neglected since leaving Yugoslavia. I figured that if I kept myself occupied, maybe I wouldn't be so annoyed by my neighbor. Maybe I would forget about her altogether. Problem was, she continued to get up to go to the bathroom every half hour or so. Her bladder must have been the size of a thimble.

Finally, after her fifth or sixth trip to the bathroom, she came back shaking her head, which I read as an apology of sorts. "Okay, I'll admit, I have a bladder infection. My boyfriend isn't circumcised. You know what I mean?"

I raised my hands to fend her off. "Please. That's too much information. I don't want to know."

She shot me a dirty look.

"How about this. Why don't we change seats? That way you won't have to crawl over me every time you have to go to the bathroom?"

Nice try, but Ellie was indignant: "Oh, so you just want my seat? You don't even care that my pee-pee is red and swollen! Nice guy!"

"You mean my seat," I replied, avoiding any comment on her red and swollen pee-pee.

This time the flight attendant looked pissed. "What's the problem now?" she asked, standing in the aisle with her hands on her hips.

"He's an ass-hole! That's the problem!" explained Ellie.

"Please, miss, keep your voice down. We have children on board."

"Only if he apologizes."

"Apologize for what?" I asked, flabbergasted, looking to the flight attendant for support.

"For not caring about my bladder infection."

"You have a bladder infection? Oh, great!" the flight attendant muttered.

"Well...let's both apologize and make up. Let's be friends again. I'm Ellie."

"James," I said, extending my hand.

The harried flight attendant gave Ellie and I a look of incredulity, shook her head, and then rushed off to attend to other needs.

Before either of us could say anything and violate our truce, which I figured was inevitable, given the volatility of our previous exchanges, I excused myself and walked to the back of the plane, looking for a bathroom or an exit, some way to hide or escape from Ellie. I was that desperate.

The flight attendant caught me as I came out of the bathroom. "Do me a favor, go easy on the girl. She's only eighteen."

So that explained Ellie's behavior. Sort of. She was still a teenager.

Following the flight attendant's request, I decided to put on a smiley face and return to my seat with a new resolve to be kind and gracious to Ellie. As it happened I didn't have to be too kind or too gracious because by this time Ellie had turned toward the window, having decided to ignore me. I took the opportunity to close my eyes and try to fall asleep, but it seemed that every time I nodded off my head would jerk to the side and snap back as 18-year-old Ellie brushed past me on her way to the bathroom, dragging her red and swollen pee-pee over my lap.

Eventually, after hours of fitful sleep, I woke up just as our plane landed in Montreal. About half of the passengers on board exited. Those of us who were continuing on to Chicago had to stay on the plane for what was supposed to be a brief twenty-minute stopover. But twenty minutes turned into forty and then sixty, when finally the captain came on over the P.A. system and announced that there had been a bomb threat and that all checked luggage would have to be re-screened. Sure enough, when we looked out the window, we saw dozens of suitcases spread out on the tarmac, where Air France personnel and airport security guards were examining each suitcase with dogs and hand-held scanning devices. Looking for a terrorist bomb.

Apparently, intelligence officials in North America and Europe were on high alert. Just one week later the Palestinian group known as Black September broke into the Israeli dormitory at Olympic Village in Munich and took eleven Israeli athletes, coaches, and officials hostage. Two hostages who resisted were killed immediately. The other nine hostages died in a botched rescue attempt carried out by German authorities after an eighteen-hour standoff.

"Oh, great," Ellie said. "I hate Montreal!"

Given the situation, I couldn't disagree.

To amuse herself and pass the time, Ellie suggested we sing Burt Bacharach songs. I declined, not because I disliked Burt Bacharach's music but because I had the world's worst voice, but Ellie jumped right in: "What... do you get...when you fall...in love?" And so on. She sang every song in the Bacharach catalogue at least once. Every so often she waved her hat and bounced up and down in her seat as though she were lap dancing.

Two hours later our plane finally took off without exploding in mid air. And we landed in Chicago, three hours after that, without exploding. "Better safe than sorry," was our captain's parting comment. I wasn't so sure it was an either/or situation. I was both safe and sorry.

"Thank you," the flight attendant said as we made our way toward the front exit, nodding at Ellie and I. The look of relief on her face said it all: she was glad to be rid of us, her two troublemakers.

Ellie was all smiles, doing a little dance step as she stepped out of the plane onto the ramp. When she danced her blond curls fluffed out from under her pork pie hat, making her look even younger than eighteen.

As we exited the plane she tapped me on the shoulder. "Say—you wanna get something to eat, a burger or maybe a pizza?"

I thanked her but said I had to catch a bus.

Ellie looked offended. Again. "Okay, loser! OR–VWAR!"

Welcome home.

L incoln. November 7, 1972

On election eve we decided to ignore the predictions of a Nixon landslide and hold a victory party at our apartment, a sprawling, multi-level flat on the top floor of a dilapidated frame house that the health department tried every year to condemn. Somehow our landlord, a retired family doctor, managed to get a special dispensation in order to keep the wrecking ball at bay for one more year, despite the fact that the windows didn't open, the radiators didn't work, and the only 'fire escape' was a hand-made wooden staircase on the outside of the house that attached to a double window in our living room, the only window that actually opened. Our furniture was Salvation Army hand-me-down from the former tenants, a rock band of ill repute whose members had been forced to go underground as a result of a series of legal problems, most of them drug-related. We had two bedrooms and an open living room that served as a flop-house for a motley assortment of guests, not all of them invited. It was, as our friends never failed to remind us, an eyesore. In spite of all that, my roommate Dennis and I loved the place dearly.

I'd wasted most of the afternoon playing contract Bridge with Joe and Faye and my friend Susie, who was a Bridge fanatic and much better than the rest of us. We played on a red plastic footstool, at least three feet in diameter, which served as a makeshift card table. Every few hands Joe would roll a number from his stash of weed and pass it around. My friend Ross, just back from Edinburgh where he'd been living with some Scottish friends, sat on the piano bench watching Susie play her hands, trying to learn from a real expert. Susie had a ferociously quick temper and no patience for Bridge fools, especially me when, like today, I happened to be her partner.

Often, Susie would fling her cards down on the footstool and say something subtle like, "Why the fuck did you bid three no trump on that hand, you ass!" Then she'd turn to Ross: "You want to play? Why don't you take Wilson's place?"

"I don't know how to play," Ross would usually say, afraid to be Susie's partner.

"Neither does Wilson."

The next to arrive was Joe and Faye's English friend Andy, who I'd last seen in Pula during our infamous last supper. A graduate teaching assistant in the art department, Andy described himself as an ex-patriot fleeing from the rigid class structure in England, which we all found ironic because he hailed from a family wealthy enough to keep a 60-foot yacht and crew year-round in Greece. As usual, Andy brought with him three of his art groupies, undergraduate art students who loved his English accent and long curly hair and followed him anywhere, mostly to his bed. Andy had his pick of the undergraduates, fucking whomever he wanted, whenever he wanted. "Greetings everyone. Instead of booze, I bring you gifts from Owsley the chemist...that's right, tabs of acid! Help yourselves, lads and lasses." He placed his acid tabs on top of the piano, popped a tab, and washed it down with a sip from Ross' beer. "Now I'm ready for a Yankee election. Bring on the clowns."

When the network news hour arrived, Dennis and his girlfriend Vicki turned on the television, flipping channels until they found Walter Cronkite's friendly face. Might as well get the bad news from Uncle Walter. While we watched, the sexy young woman from the efficiency apartment below came up the stairs with a plate of her special brownies. Mostly Heather kept to herself, coming up only rarely and then only for parties or hook-ups. I always had the distinct feeling that Heather didn't like us much, but I never knew exactly why. I suspected Dennis, who was a notorious philanderer. Might it have been an attempted seduction gone awry? Following Heather were a few stragglers and freeloaders, most of whom I had never seen before.

Optimists all, we'd prepared for a long evening of election coverage by stocking up on supplies, mostly alcohol and drugs, so you can imagine our shock and dismay when we discovered at the top of the hour, only eight p.m. Eastern Standard Time, that Nixon was projected to win by over 20 percentage points. Reportedly, all three networks were preparing to call the race and by implication relay the message that all McGovern supporters could go fuck themselves. Old Tricky Dick had done it again, riding the Law and Order wave of the Southern Democrats who had abandoned their party by the millions when ole LBJ, fucking traitor, had signed all them there Civil Rights laws. Whose country was this, anyway? Mob rule, fueled by racism and nationalism and a particularly American brand of resentment.

"A landslide of historic proportions," said Walter, or something to that effect. So just like that our victory party, even before we could drink enough alcohol or drop enough acid to get it rolling properly, was squashed, fucked, Nixoned.

"Turn off the TV!" someone shouted.

"Grab the fucker and throw it out the window!" someone else shouted.

It took Dennis a few minutes to tame the rowdies. He stood between them and his television, saying in a calm, therapeutic voice, "Now, no one's going to throw the TV out the window. Let's all relax and see what happens, okay?"

Just then McGovern came on the screen. He looked as though he were about to concede, or cry, or piss his pants.

Before McGovern could finish speaking, we heard Andy scream from the back bedroom, where he'd been fooling around with one of his groupies. "My God, look at that face...don't you see...it's splotched. He's a leper! He's a fucking leper!"

With that, Andy ran screaming through the living room and jumped out the window onto the rickety fire escape, half running, half falling down the steps. By the time he hit bottom he'd taken more than his fair share of rotten timber with him.

Andy ran off down the street howling, "Owwwwww...me arse is full of splinters!"

Not far behind, one of Andy's amorous groupies hobbled out of the bedroom after him, jeans and panties pulled down to her ankles, all bare ass and bush from the waist down. "Balls!" She bent over to pull up her pants, giving us a full view of her gorgeous ass, and then followed Andy out the window and down the fire escape.

From that point on, our victory celebration turned surreal. When a gloating, glowering Nixon came on the TV screen, all swarthy skin and flabby jowls, even serious-minded Dennis had had enough of Nixon's rants (four more years...peace with honor...Watergate, who me?). Dennis turned off the sound and put a Rolling Stones album on the stereo, blaring "Paint it Black" over the speakers: "I see a red door and I want it painted black / No colors anymore I want them to turn black..."

No one was more depressed than Joe. "Now pot will never be legalized. Fucking McGovern would have to blow it."

"Deal the cards," Susie said, exasperated. "Who gives a damn about the election? Did you really think McGovern would win? He's a moron!"

"Yeah, okay, but wait a minute, man...let me finish this first." He took a roach clip out of his pocket and fired up what was left of his latest number.

"Fuck! Doesn't anybody here want to play Bridge?"

"Aye, but lighten up, first things first," Ross said, taking the roach from Joe.

Ghostly images flickered on the TV screen, casting dancing shadows on the wall, black and white stick figures gesticulating furtively: McGovern conceding, Nixon accepting, pundits pontificating on the death of the hippie, anti-war, pot-smoking, McCarthy, McGovern, leftist coalition. Only the mob left standing, the lowest common denominator, right out of Pap in Huck Finn and a hundred other American Ur texts. All to the sound of the Rolling Stones: "It's not easy facin' up when your whole world is black."

It was the end of the dream: there would be no peace in our lifetime. In my mind's eye, as on a screen, I saw images of Martin Luther King, Jr., dying on a motel balcony in Memphis, of Bobby Kennedy dying on the floor of the Ambassador Hotel in Los Angeles, of anti-war protesters being beaten bloody in the streets of Chicago, of villages burning and soldiers dying in the rice paddies of Vietnam, images shot through with smoke and flames, a decade of bleeding, dying, burning, this is the end my friend, apocalypse now.

After a while, my head spinning, I excused myself and went to bed, depressed and exhausted. I fell on the bed fully clothed and was about to fall asleep when I heard my bedroom door open and the muffled sound of sandals crossing the wooden floor. "Want a brownie?" my downstairs neighbor Heather asked, sitting on the mattress beside me and running her hand between my thighs. I could feel the heat from her body and smell the patchouli oil on her bare skin.

"Hey, thanks, but I need to sleep right now. I'm not feeling so well...I think I'm going to be sick."

"Maybe this will help." Heather stood up and took off her India print dress, pulling it over her long blond hair and revealing the naked curves of a luscious body that, under normal circumstances, would be to die for. I knew, from past experience, what carnal pleasures could be found there.

"Nice tits."

The last thing I remember was reaching out my hand to squeeze one of her magnificent round breasts. To the best of my knowledge, my hand never reached its target.

Much later I was awakened when someone knocked on my bedroom door and then opened it slightly. "Wilson, are you awake? I could spend the night...if you want?" Susie whispered.

"Oh, yeah...that'd be great...but I think I'll just crash. I'm really exhausted tonight."

Well, then, fuck off!" Susie snapped.

Waking up the next morning I found an empty beer bottle stuck between my legs and a broken plate of brownies dropped on the floor. My nocturnal visitors had not gone gently into the night.

L incoln. December 23, 1972

"You're kidding, right?" That was Joe's reaction when I told him Chantal was coming to visit for two weeks over Christmas. We were having coffee in the student union at the university, where Joe was waiting for a babe from the art apartment, one of Andy's castoffs, who he had been pursuing for a couple of weeks. He liked art department chicks. As Joe said, it was easy to get them into bed and they didn't cling to you afterwards as if you were some kind of Big Daddy.

I gave him a dirty look. "No. Why would I be kidding?"

"I mean, what self-respecting French chick would come all this way just to get laid? She's hot, a really nice piece, so how could she be that desperate? Love the one you're with, man...just like the song says. That's always been my motto."

I raised my hand and said, "Joe...you have a way of reducing everything to the lowest common denominator."

"What? Getting laid? You know what your problem is, man? You're too cerebral...and too prissy."

"Yeah, well, I really like her."

"Man, that's the same exact thing you said about the last love of your life, I can't remember her name. Julie, right?"

"Fuck you."

"Whatever."

The night before I flew to New York to meet Chantal, Joe took me to Casey's bar, just the two of us, partly to make amends for what he admitted was his earlier 'insensitivity' in the student union and partly to find out what I was planning to do about Chantal. Despite our differences, Joe was one of my best friends and had been for years. After our beers came, he asked: "So, James...are you, like, thinking about marriage or something permanent like that?"

I shrugged. "I don't know."

"So you really dig this chick?"

"That's what I've been trying to tell you. The problem is, you never listen."

Joe took a long drink from his draft, adjusted his granny glasses, and spoke slowly in a serious tone of voice, or as serious as Joe could get. "We're here to talk about your problem, James," he said. "It's clear to me now that we need to have the *marriage* talk, even if it cost me your friendship, which it might, given your prissy attitude, which by the way I blame on the French chick. You need to smoke more weed, like you used to back in the day when you ran around mostly with hippie chicks like Julie. So here's the thing, man. I have to warn you...it's not easy being married. I mean, can you imagine having sex with the same person for the rest of your life? You see where I'm coming from? It's a bummer."

I ignored him.

"Look around you, man," Joe said, waving his arms. "Look at all the available pussy! So much flesh! Who could settle for just one chick?"

"I don't know. Chantal and I are very compatible."

"You know what I think? I think you're compatible because neither one of you can understand half of what the other person is saying. You don't even have to worry about tuning each other out–you're already tuned out!"

I had to laugh at this. "Probably so. And what about you? You and Faye seem to have done okay."

Joe finished his beer and asked for another. "Yeah, I suppose, but I have to be honest with you, James...Faye and I mix it up sometimes...you know, do some swapping with other couples...just to keep it fresh...or as fresh as it can be after five, six years."

I was a bit taken aback by this, even though I knew Joe had his difficulties with the concept of fidelity. "Really? I always thought you and Faye were the ideal couple, good friends and lovers, solid as a rock."

"But see, that's your thing, man. Fidelity or monogamy or whatever you call it. We, on the other hand, try to have an open marriage. I get a little on the side, and so does Faye. No harm, no foul. We both like to keep it fresh, and believe me, fucking other people is the only way you can keep a marriage fresh. I should know, man."

"Faye gets a little on the side? I don't believe it."

"It's true. You know Andy, that crazy English motherfucker from the art department?

"Faye and Andy?"

He nodded. "Sure. They've been fucking for years. So what? I don't care. It keeps her from saying anything about my affairs. Although I'd be less than honest if I didn't say that sometimes I wish she'd pick someone less objectionable than that fucking Andy."

"I thought you liked Andy."

"No way. It's Faye who likes him, not me. The fucker tried to drown me on the way to Trieste, right after we left you guys in Pula. You missed all the action, man. After we left Pula, Andy got pissed because he thought I was using more than my share of the communal drugs, which may or may not have been true. I mean, who was counting? And actually, I was the one who should have been pissed, because Faye and Andy were fucking the entire trip."

Here he paused and shook his head, like shaking off a bad memory. "Anyway, what was I saying?"

"You were going to tell me about how Andy tried to drown you."

"Oh yeah...Andy tried to drown me. This happened two days out of

Pula, on our way to Trieste. We were all pretty stoned, especially me, I'll admit. I was out on the sundeck doing yoga. Well, okay, not really yoga. Actually I was zonked, lying on a yoga mat and catching some rays. When I tried to stand up to go get a cold beer and a bottle of sunscreen, someone who must have been Andy (who else could it have been?) pushed me from behind. I didn't have a fighting chance, man...and as I fell headfirst over the side of the yacht I heard this sadistic fucking laugh behind me. I lost my sunglasses when I hit the water, so I couldn't see a thing, nothing, as I splashed around in the ocean yelling for help. Finally Faye heard me yelling from the other side of the yacht and came over to take a look. 'Help! Throw me a rope or something, Andy pushed me over the side!' I was screaming. 'Oh, get back on board, you asshole,' she said, tossing me a life preserver. Just then Andy came running on deck waving the leather satchel where he kept his drugs and bellowing: 'You motherfucker, you dropped all the acid... you fucking acid freak!'"

By now I was laughing so hard I could barely hear Joe's tale of woe and treachery.

"I'd never seen Andy so pissed. He took the wheel from Danny and steered a sharp left, toward Venice, and left me thrashing about in the water with nothing in sight but waves, one after another, trying to drown me. I don't know how long I was out there by myself, but soon enough I started hallucinating. Yeah, I saw these big fish, swimming all around me. Man, they were all the colors of the rainbow, bright psychedelic colors, red and blue and yellow and green, like neon lights flashing under the water. And the fish all had big white mouths and puffy lips, blowing bubbles and looking at me with their fish eyes. I freaked, man. I thought I was a goner for sure. Maybe a half hour later the yacht came back in sight, now bearing right down on me, trying to run me over. I dived down as deep as I could to escape that crazy English bastard, but in the confusion I lost my life preserver and came to the surface coughing and sputtering. By then someone on the yacht had dropped anchor, because the boat was pitching and bobbing no more than 100 feet away. I swam over to the side, where Faye had a rope waiting. 'Will you get on board, you moron!' she said. So I climbed aboard, looking around for Andy, only to be told that Andy had locked himself in his cabin with the drug satchel, where he stayed for twenty-four hours straight. Even when he came out, the next day, he refused to talk to me. He didn't say another word to me the rest of the trip, which was fine by me. What a royal English prick!"

"Jesus...I had no idea, I thought you were best friends," was all I could manage, trying to bring my laughing under control, which took a few seconds. When I was more composed I told him I had to get home to pack a suitcase for my flight to New York the next morning.

"Why are you flying to New York?" he asked.

"To meet Chantal. She doesn't speak English, remember?"

"So? She can get on a plane, can't she...even if she is French."

"Whatever," I said, leaving him to wait for his art department babe.

I didn't see Joe again until the day after Christmas. He called that morning and invited Chantal and I to dinner that evening.

I was a little nervous when we knocked on the door of Joe and Fay's apartment, worried about what Joe might say to offend Chantal. I thought Chantal might still be pissed because of what happened in Pula, when during our meal together there, Andy and the boys had gotten drunk and rowdy and made her sing the Beatles' song "Yesterday" before they would let her leave the restaurant and go back to our room.

But when I opened the door, Joe said, "*Bonjour*, yesterday,"

Chantal smiled. "*Bonjour*, walrus." Then she stepped into the apartment and kissed Joe on the cheek.

L incoln. December 27, 1972

The evening started off badly thanks to Joe, or as Faye referred to him that night, her soon-to-be ex-husband. Faye looked her knockout best, with pale skin, bedroom eyes, and dark frizzy hair, wearing a tight white sweater and black pumps. Joe wore the same jeans and tee-shirt he always wore and looked like he hadn't shaved in several days. Even before we had time to hang up our coats, Joe wanted to bring out the drugs. "Hey, Chantal...*voulez vous*...get stoned?" he asked, trying to show off his French but only showing off the fact that he'd wasted two years of French classes at the university.

Chantal turned to me. "*La drogue?*"

"*Si...marijuana.*"

"*Non, merci*," she said back to Joe. "*Je préfére le vin rouge.*"

Joe grinned. "Maybe she's straight," he said, as if she weren't standing right there in front of him. He just didn't get it. Not everyone liked to get stoned all the time.

So we moved into the living room, where Joe made a big deal about sitting next to Chantal so he could "practice his French," as he put it. The only French he practiced was putting his arm around her shoulders and squeezing her tits. Faye pretended not to notice his lechery. She brought in glasses and a bottle of red wine and let us help ourselves. After a few minutes of bullshit conversation about the weather and memories of Yugoslavia, what a fine time it was and all that crap, we fell into the silence of the language impaired, with only me being able to communicate with everyone sitting around the coffee table.

Finally Chantal broke the silence. She asked what she thought was a simple question. "She wants to know what you do," I said.

"Do?" Joe asked. "What do you mean?"

"Your profession. Your *métier*. What you do for a living."

Joe looked at me for help. I didn't offer any. What could I say that could possibly explain what he did for a living?

"Well, funny you should ask about that. See, I used to be a graduate student, a teaching assistant in the philosophy department at the university, until I dropped out of school last year...too much stress, you know, trying to take classes and teach an undergraduate class at the same time...very stressful...and taking too much speed, I'll admit...because I was so stressed and, well, stress is bad for the heart, you know...and it also causes cancer, I think.." Here Joe lost his train of thought, or his interest in finishing his sentence.

So I jumped in and said, "He was teaching an undergraduate class on Kant's *Critique of Pure Reason*. Do you know the German philosopher Immanuel Kant?"

"Cunt! I call him Immanuel cunt," Joe said, laughing at his own joke. How many dozens of times had I heard that joke?

"Cunt?" Chantal asked.

"Yeah, translate that, James," Joe said, amused.

"Uh...*il disait....la chatte...c'est une connerie*," I stammered.

Chantal pointed at Joe. "*Le philosophe de la chatte? C'est vrai?*"

Everyone laughed.

"Right on, sister," I said. "That's about the only thing he's a philosopher of...pussy and pot, mostly pot these days."

"*Autrefois le philosophe de la chatte...mais maintenant qu'est-ce qu'il fait?*" Chantal asked again.

"Basically nothing," I said, getting the drift of her question. "He manages this building, which his father owns.

"*Rien?*" Chantal turned to me. "*Comme toi. Rien.*"

"Not exactly nothing," Joe said. "It's more like...or like..."

"Fuck it, let's eat," Faye said, putting an end to this pleasant conversation, driving a stake through its heart before it could drain the blood out of the entire evening.

We made small talk during dinner. Everyone behaved, more or less, except that between the main course and dessert and coffee Joe pushed his chair back from the table and lit a number. With Joe getting high, Faye making coffee, and me spacing out, Chantal took the opportunity to get up and put on her coat. I didn't have a clue as to what she was doing: getting some fresh air, going for a walk, catching an early flight to Paris, whatever. Finally I went to the door as if to follow, but Chantal held up her hand to stop me and said she'd be right back. With that, she stepped outside and disappeared into the night.

I closed the door. "She says she wants to go for a walk by herself."

"Why?" Faye asked. "Who would want to walk at night in this shitty neighborhood?"

"Don't worry about it," Joe said. "She probably just has gas. Sometimes I have that effect on chicks. Not intentional."

Faye shot him an evil look, annoyed. I could begin to see the friction in their relationship. There were times when she seemed more like Joe's mother than his wife, a parent that had to supervise her miscreant of a son.

Rock solid, Faye clearly was the foundation of their marriage.

Who knows, maybe Chantal did have gas, because she returned five minutes later saying she felt much better. So we finished dessert and coffee and then, while Joe tried to converse with Chantal on the sofa, Faye and I did the dishes. We watched them from the kitchen, Joe stammering in French ("*Qu'est-ce que...votre...*") and Chantal trying to decode what Walrus was saying.

Faye and I had an opportunity to talk while we did the dishes. "Joe told me about what happened on the way to Trieste, after you guys left Pula," I said. "How Andy or someone pushed him off the yacht and he almost drowned. I had no idea."

"Ha! Is that what he told you?" Faye asked, snorting. "He's so full of shit. Let me tell you what really happened. He was stoned out of his mind that day, so stoned that he stumbled and fell over the side of the yacht all by his lonesome. He started yelling for help and thrashing around in the water, but he was too stoned to swim twenty feet to the boat. Even after we threw him a rope, it took fifteen minutes for him to find it and grab hold. We had to keep tossing the rope until it hit him in the face. When we finally managed to pull him on board, he was crying like a baby and saying someone tried to drown him."

"So Andy didn't..."

"No, why would Andy try to drown Joe? Joe's no threat to Andy, believe me."

"Does that mean you and Andy are..."

"Yeah, but that has nothing to do with Joe. And he doesn't care. He has his own indiscretions, mostly with students or the skanks he meets at Casey's. Look at him with Chantal. He wishes!"

We left early, before Joe could bring out the hard drugs. Chantal seemed bored, and I wanted to get her away from Joe and off to bed, since we only had a few more days together before Chantal returned to France.

On our way out Faye stopped me at the door. "Watch out," she whispered in my ear. "She'll break your heart."

L incoln. January 3, 1973

That comment worried me for the rest of Chantal's visit. I wanted to attribute Faye's cynicism to her own personal experience of being married to Joe, for whom monogamy was a dirty word. No, it couldn't be easy being married to a free love philanderer like Joe. He embraced the new attitude toward sex and sexual partners: the more, the merrier, no questions asked, and no feelings of guilt or remorse. Joe and Andy and most of their friends would never let what they considered an arrangement of convenience get in the way of casual sex with strangers, which was better and surely more exciting than boring married sex.

So finally on the last day of her visit Chantal and I had 'the talk.' What's to become of us? What now?

We were sitting side by side on our bedraggled sofa. Chantal shook her head and then launched in on what turned out to be her most animated speech, ever. Translated, it went something like this: "Hippies! You and your friends...all of them are hippies! No jobs, no professions, no plans for the future. I don't know how they live or where they get the money to travel, because that's all they seem to do, travel. Not only you, but Joe and Faye and their English friend Andy. Then there's your friend Ross, who spends half the year in Heidelberg with one group of soccer hooligans and the other half of the year in Edinburgh with another group of soccer hooligans. Occasionally he resurfaces here to visit friends and family. Nomads, all of them homeless and perpetually on the go, either traveling between continents or planning the next trip, looking for what? I don't get it.

"Drugs everywhere. They're all dopers, especially Joe and Andy and that art department group. They smoke pot constantly, but they also experiment with the harder stuff, hashish and opium and speed and acid, who knows what else? New Years Eve Andy dropped acid and jumped off the fire escape. We never found out if he hurt himself or not, because he went crawling off in the darkness barking like a dog. A dog! Who wants to deal with that? Not me.

"And truly, this apartment, in fact this whole building should be condemned as a public danger. It's a death trap. The stairway creaks and the fire escape outside collapsed long ago. To make matters worse, there's no heat from the radiators. The landlord came over yesterday to staple sheets of plastic over the windows, so now instead of cold air coming in through the cracks we have plastic sheets that flap every time the wind gusts outside.

75

It's like winter in the Alps, *sans* Alps. I'm freezing. I can't get warm, no matter how many sweaters I wear.

"Even worse than the cold and disrepair are the crazies who come up to the apartment at all hours of the day and night, looking to party. Occasionally someone will come up hoping to jam with the rock band that lived here previously. One morning we woke up to find someone sleeping on the coach who none of us had ever seen before, with two of the guy's friends passed out on the floor. One afternoon, while you were at the university registering for next semester, the young blond woman who lives on the second floor, totally naked, walked up the stairs and into the apartment without knocking. 'Is James here?' she asked, looking at me suspiciously. 'Oh, you must be the French girlfriend, yes?'

"I nodded, too shocked to respond.

"Incredibly, she walked directly up to me and placed my hand on her bare breast. Just like that. 'Let's see now,' she said, 'how does the song go... *voulez-vous couchez avec moi?*'

"Can you imagine?

"I just glared at her until she started to feel uncomfortable, turned and walked back down the stairs. 'Your loss,' she said.

"As if I'd always wanted to sleep with a tall blond woman who looked like a stick with breasts! I don't think so.

"I'm staying in a flophouse! *Un bordel!*"

Her rant lasted a good fifteen or twenty minutes, scolding me about my friends, my lifestyle, my apartment, my everything. Listening to her, you'd think I lived with a bunch of lazy, drugged out zombies, which, looking back, I have to admit wasn't too far off the mark. To her, we were a pretty ragged bunch of counterculture drop-outs. Chantal was used to a regular lifestyle, working nine months a year teaching school, a serious, sober profession. She had no interest in joining the counterculture. Or me, I was about to discover.

Last night sealed the matter, if it was ever in doubt. After we had gone to bed and started to fool around, we heard someone climbing up the fire escape outside, boards splintering and raining down the side of the building. It sounded like the whole building was crashing down. When the intruder reached the top, he pushed on the double window that opened into the living room, ripping the plastic sheet from top to bottom and sending staples flying across the room everywhere.

Chantal tried to restrain me, thinking a burglar was breaking into the apartment, but I knew no self-respecting burglar would break into this dump.

"No, it's probably just someone looking for a party," I said. I pulled on a sweater and walked into the living room. On the floor below the window sat a shaggy, bearded young man wearing a black pea coat. My friend Ross.

"Shite! I think I've ruined your window."

"Ross, what are you doing here?" I asked. "What time is it?"

"Midnight. But I brought wine!" He waved a bottle of wine. "To celebrate."

"Celebrate what?"

"Oh hell, I don't know, love and glory, the same old story...whatever." He sounded drunk. Completely drunk.

By this time Chantal was peeking around the corner to get a good look at Ross.

"Ross, this is Chantal. Chantal, Ross."

"Pleased to make yer acquaintance, m'lady," Ross said, bowing ridiculously from his sitting position and nearly falling on his nose.

I managed to close the window, torn plastic and all, preventing the gusts of cold air from freezing the three of us on the spot. Then I took the bottle of wine to the kitchen and opened it. By the time I returned Ross and Chantal were sitting on opposite sides of the room, her on the sofa, him on the stolen chair we called the throne, staring suspiciously at each other. His wet, matted hair hung down to his shoulders and over his coat collar. He looked like a derelict, a homeless person. I poured each of us each a glass of wine and set the bottle down. "Ross isn't as bad as he looks. Not quite."

"Thanks," Ross said.

"I thought you were leaving for Germany."

"Next week." He turned to me: "For the skiing."

Chantal perked up. *"Faire du ski. J'aime faire du ski."*

Ross shook his shaggy head and suddenly looked dejected and limp, as though the spirit had suddenly left his body. He slumped over, holding his head in both hands. I thought for a moment he was about to burst into tears. "Yeah, I gotta get back to Europe...I gotta get out of this place...there's nothing to do here but drink, man...I can't stop drinking...I'm killing myself...I hate this fucking place!"

I was skeptical. "But what do you do in Europe...besides skiing, and drinking?"

"Ross perked up, thinking of his life in Europe. "Lots of stuff. I stay busy because there's more to do over there. Soccer and cycling with my mates...hiking in the Black Forest in Germany or the Highlands when I'm in Scotland...touring and sightseeing...you know how it is in Europe, the cafes and the museums and the art galleries...so much to do there you can never do it all, but here all I do is drink at Casey's because there's nothing else to do in this godforsaken fucking place!"

"And I need a wooooooman," Ross wailed. "I haven't had a woman since I left Europe. I don't know why, but women in Europe like me better. They don't like me here...they won't sleep with me!"

Chantal must have gotten the drift of what he was saying because she shook her head. *"Non...je ne pense pas!"*

While Ross complained about not having anything to do here except drink, he kept on drinking red wine and refilling his glass, even though he was already too drunk to stand up. One minute he was complaining about a woman he met at Casey's who'd turned him down earlier that evening, and the next he was rambling on about Nixon and Vietnam and his fucking local draft board who kept sending him hate mail. "The motherfuckers are after me, I know it. I gotta get outta here!"

We ended up drinking the entire bottle of wine and, although I wasn't happy about it, letting Ross spend the night on the sofa. Actually, we didn't have much choice, since Ross had passed out cold, his head draped at a crazy angle over the arm of the sofa. I grabbed his feet and pulled him down flat on the sofa, and then tossed a blanket over him. Good night, sweet prince.

Then I took our empty wine bottle and stuck it between Ross's thighs. "It's a tradition here in the apartment—I'll explain later."

When we woke up this morning, the last day of Chantal's visit, Ross had already gone, who knows where. It was too early for Casey's, but I didn't worry. Wherever he went, Ross always had lots of friends, most of them male, who were willing to take him in and listen to his latest stories from the Continent, where the 'pigs' didn't hassle you and it was easy to get laid because all the fucking Puritans had been deported to the States, thank you very much.

Chantal and I went out for a late breakfast and then, for exercise, walked around the university, enjoying the sunny but cold day. The walking, fresh air, and crisp sunshine cured my headache and restored my spirits, and by the time we made it back to the apartment I was feeling frisky again. I declared that this day belonged to us and us alone, so I found a magic marker and made two Do Not Disturb signs, one of which we hung on the downstairs door to the apartment and the other on the fire escape outside. "The last thing we need now is for Joe to come over with his weed, or Andy with his stash of acid," I said, locking the door and barricading the fire escape window. "Let's get lost, let's drop out of sight."

So drop out we did, as day plunged into frigid night, and the wind and the snow howled outside and lashed the side of the frame house, swaying the timbers ever so slightly.

I sensed the finality of this day. Even then, I sensed I would never see Chantal again. A chapter in my life was coming to an end.

We sat at the kitchen table staring at each other over a plate of sliced ham, cheese, and fruit. The kitchen was freezing because it was cut off from the rest of the apartment by the stairwell, far away from the nearest radiator. The one window in the kitchen was frosted over with a layer of white powder. The walls felt like ice when you happened to touch them. It was like living in an ice cave. We were so cold our teeth started clattering.

"*Viens, j'ai un idée,*" I said, taking Chantal's hand and leading her down the hall into the bathroom, where I drew a hot bath and poured in half a bottle of bubble bath. We stripped off our clothes and dropped them on the bathroom floor, which was as cold as the kitchen walls. Like walking on a block of ice. Then, holding hands, we stepped into a sea of bubbling foam. As soon as I sank into the warm water, we started to relax. A cloud of hot steam filled the small, enclosed bathroom and fogged the mirror and the small window above the bathtub.

I pulled Chantal up onto my lap. "*Essayons la baise sous l'eau*," I said, laughing. But when she tried to straddle me, water splashed over the side of the bathtub and pooled on the already cracked linoleum floor, so much water that I suggested we move to the bedroom.

Laughing, we ran from the bathroom into the bedroom, across the cold, creaking wooden floor, with an arctic wind howling outside, flapping the sheets of plastic stapled over the windows. We'd come full circle, from the warmth of an Adriatic summer to the frozen tundra of a North American winter. Though I was cold and still dripping, I wanted her now as much as I had wanted her back in the heat of Strasbourg or Trieste or Pula.

L incoln. January 4, 1973

We hardly said a word on the drive to the airport. There was nothing left to say, really, except goodbye, hope to see you in June. Joe and Faye offered to give us a ride to the airport, so we sat huddled together in the back seat of their Volvo. Chantal seemed totally withdrawn into herself, unavailable, inscrutable. Joe made small talk and joked about American culture (or lack thereof) and Andy's misbehavior in Yugoslavia, trying to find a way to lift the gloomy mood that had settled over all four of us, even Faye, who seemed every bit as distant as Chantal.

At the airport we checked Chantal's suitcase and then walked slowly to the gate. With every step the feeling of *déjà vu* got stronger. Chantal turned to look at me but said nothing. It was as though we were retracing our footsteps from last August, when we'd said goodbye at the Strasbourg train station, except this time she was the one leaving. Minutes later the plane started boarding, so we didn't have much time for sweet farewells. She hugged me, I kissed her neck, and then she turned and walked to the gate, looking back at the very last instant before disappearing into the tunnel with the other passengers. And then she was gone.

"Sir, are you okay?" a woman at the check-in counter asked me.

"Oh...sorry," I stammered. "Just saying goodbye."

She smiled, knowingly, as I walked back toward the terminal. No doubt she'd seen such sweet sorrow a thousand times before. It was a common occurrence, so what was my problem? Time to suck it up and get on with my life.

When I caught up with Joe and Faye, who were waiting for me curbside, I collapsed in the back seat of their Volvo without saying a word.

"You seem bummed out, James," Faye said.

"Yeah, you look fucking morose," Joe added with his usual bluntness. "Are you okay or what?"

"I just don't have a good feeling about her leaving...it's not like last time..."

"Hey man, maybe I should fire up a number. What do you say? You want?" Joe asked.

Faye shot him a dirty look.

"Not for me." The thought of getting high this early in the morning, under these circumstances, made me want to vomit.

Instead, I sat slouched on the back seat of the Volvo, brooding on Chantal's visit and trying to figure out what had gone wrong. In my heart I knew what had gone wrong, of course, but just then I did not have the fortitude to face up to the truth. Though she hadn't actually said as much, she clearly seemed disappointed and not very impressed with what she'd seen of America. She lacked the spark, the *joie de vivre* that I'd seen in Europe. I could tell she hadn't enjoyed her stay, especially spending time with my crazy hippie friends, but I didn't know exactly what that foretold about our future. In Strasbourg we'd parted on such a high note, with such euphoria, that it was easy to project our relationship into the future. Now I wasn't so sure. I couldn't shake the feeling that I would never see Chantal again, either in Europe or America.

When Joe pulled up in front of 1631 F, he switched off the motor and turned around to face me. "Come on, James, cheer up. You'll see her again, man. Don't worry about it. She'll be back." He reached over the seat and gave my shoulder a squeeze.

"He's right," Faye said. "You'll see her in Strasbourg this summer. Just like you planned."

Though I didn't really believe them, I was moved by their effort to console me. "Yeah, thanks, I suppose you're right. We plan to go to Greece in July."

Before I could open the car door, Joe took a joint out of his pocket and handed it to me. "For later."

"Thanks. I'll probably need it."

Once I stepped out of the Volvo and closed the door, I started to feel lonely again, abandoned. But as I climbed the stairs to our apartment, I heard voices and laughter and the inimitable sound of Susie yelling. Cheered by their rowdiness, I followed the voices up into the living room and found Susie yelling at my friend Alan, who'd just arrived back in town, while Dennis and Vicki roared with laughter. Alan looked a lot like Ross, with shoulder-length hair and full beard, except Alan always wore an enormous pair of hiking boots with red shoelaces as thick as rope that were more appropriate for climbing Mount Everest than walking around a city or sitting in a living room.

Alan had moved to Santa Fe the previous summer and had been trying to persuade me to join him in New Mexico as a kind of two-person writer's colony, even though neither of us had published a word other than reviews and juvenile fiction in the university student newspaper, sentimental crap that no one aside from our friends ever bothered to read. I'd kept putting him off, saying I was going to Europe for the summer, maybe forever. He had come home for Christmas but ended up staying longer than expected because, as usual, he'd run out of money for the return bus ticket. He was visiting all his friends and family members, hoping for handouts to pay for a Greyhound bus ticket back to his current one-person writer's colony in Santa Fe.

"Susie, listen, you're a piss-poor teacher, you don't have any patience," Alan was saying, pleading with Susie to stay calm. "You should hear yourself."

"That's because you're a fucking imbecile!" Susie shouted back. "Nobody could teach you how to play Bridge. You're too stupid!"

I could tell Susie was on edge, more than her usual level of agitation, by the way she paced back and forth from the fire escape to the piano, a tall lanky woman with doe-like legs and short-cropped hair, a bona-fide tomboy. Suddenly she spotted me, which usually meant I was the one about to be yelled at. I felt like the proverbial deer caught in headlights. "Thank God! Wilson can be our fourth. I'll even take him as my partner...even that asshole plays better than you do."

Susie scowled at Alan, who tried to ignore her. He gave me a hug as I walked into the room and said, "Good to see you, man." Then he pulled me aside and whispered, "Susie pisses me off."

"You're not the only one," I said. "But she's a hell of a Bridge player. Here, light this for me." I handed him the joint Joe had given me earlier.

"Don't mind if I do."

Alan lit the number while Susie dealt the cards. Dennis and Vicki sat opposite one another smirking and leaving me to look across the footstool into the furious, unforgiving eyes of Susie, my sometime friend, sometime antagonist, and Bridge guru.

The best strategy when playing with a maniac like Susie, I'd discovered the hard way, was to let her do all the bidding. So I reminded myself to keep my mouth shut and follow her lead. No matter how many points I had in my hand, I would nod my head and smile moronically, waiting for her to decide what to bid. Even then I usually managed to fuck things up, play the wrong card or make the wrong counterbid. Partly it was the tension that came when playing with a card control freak like Susie. I was so afraid of screwing up that I always screwed up and then had to face the wrath of Susie.

"Hey, Wilson, you missed the excitement this afternoon–Heather came up to see you," Dennis said. "She baked a carrot cake for you."

"For me? I thought she didn't like us."

"That's not true," Vicki said, correcting me. With raven black hair, bushy eyebrows, and dark glasses, Vicki was the smartest person in the room, wherever she went. She was also the most sarcastic. "She just doesn't like Dennis. You, she finds fascinating. I think she's madly in love with you. You don't realize that having a French girlfriend has real cachet. She's jealous of Chantal, it's obvious. She wants what she can't have. It's basic psychology. If you tried, said some dirty French words to her, *baise-moi ma cherie*, you could be her French lover boy. I bet she'd put on a French maid's uniform and prance around naked on all fours. Come on, *Monsieur* Wilson, wouldn't you like to see that blond head of hers bobbing up and down under your sheets?"

Dennis laughed. "Vicki doesn't like blondes. She feels threatened. It's part of her Greek heritage: the fear of blondes. I call it blondophobia."

"What? Why would I not like blondes?" Vicki protested. "Let me be clear, I do not dislike blondes, even if they do tend to be vapid and enjoy their rightful place as sex objects. Actually, Dennis has a thing for blondes. He's always wanted to sleep with one, but every blonde he's ever known has turned him down. Poor baby, you'll probably never see a blond snatch, ever."

"Including Heather?" I asked. "Did she turn you down?"

Dennis shook his head. "I'm afraid I'll have to take the Fifth on that one."

"Aha...I thought so! That's why she's been pissed off at us all this time. You fucking tried to seduce her!"

"And failed miserably," Vicki said.

"Enough psychology, let's play cards," Susie said. "And by the way, I'm only playing with Wilson for the first rubber. After that, you guys flip a coin. It's no fair that I always get stuck with Wilson."

"Even though he has a French girlfriend?"

"I'm not impressed...unless she plays Bridge better than he does."

"Hey, I'm right here! You're talking about me as if I weren't even here."

"So when do I get to meet this French babe?" Alan asked, passing the joint to Dennis.

"Too late. I put her on the plane today."

"What a shame!" Vicki snorted. "French babe meets mountain man. What a pair you two would make. Watch out, Wilson, you have competition. You might lose your cachet."

Alan turned to me. "Is she making fun of me?"

"It would appear so," I said.

"And where on God's green earth did you find such a stylish pair of boots? Not even Wilson can compete with those boots."

Later, after Susie more or less won the first rubber by herself, with no help from me, her mute partner, Dennis and I went out for cold beer and snacks. By the time we returned Alan had disappeared, running away, we imagined, from Susie's temper and Vicki's sarcasm. Who could blame him? We played another rubber, chicks versus cats, and after Susie and Vicki embarrassed us by winning the rubber in three consecutive hands, I tossed my cards on the footstool and declared that I'd had enough abuse for one night and didn't want to play any more Bridge ever, as long as I lived.

"Pussy!" Susie said.

"Speaking of which, I think I'll go down and try a piece of that carrot cake."

"Piece of what?" Vicki asked.

Dennis laughed. "I hear the cream cheese frosting is mighty tasty on the tongue."

"As if you'll ever find out," Vicki scoffed, as I grabbed my beer and walked out of the living room, cheered by my crazy friends and their high spirits.

Whatever happened with Chantal, life wouldn't wait. Life beckoned me down the stairs and around the corner to Heather's door. What had Joe said that day in the student union? Love the one you're with, or something to that effect. Maybe Joe wasn't just a pot-head.

Maybe he was, truly, *le philosophe de la chatte.*

S trasbourg, France. May 18, 1973

James,

Peut-être vas-tu me prendre pour une idiote, une insensée, une ingrate mais le fait est là—je suis terriblement "mordue" par les voyages—je viens de connaître une association qui organise des voyages en Afghanistan et Indes pour deux mois au prix incroyable de 2,000 à 2,800 F (tout compris, meme l'avian aller et retour)—je'nai pas resister à la tentation de m'y inscrire—le grèce n'a plus d'attrait pour moi—si ce voyage t'interesse ausi, ecris moi vite un petit mot—les places sont très limiteés—toutes mes penseés.

—Chantal

PART 3 / SANTA FE

The author's teepee on Nine Mile Road, Santa Fe, 1975 (photograph by author).

L incoln, May 23, 1973

An idiot? An insensate? An ingrate? That and a few other choice names I yelled out after opening Chantal's letter, kicking the footstool across the living room and then stomping around the apartment for a few furious minutes while trying to calm down. Fortunately I was alone, so I didn't make an ass of myself in front of my friends.

In short, I was pissed. I wanted to go to India and Afghanistan about as much as I wanted to go to Siberia or Outer Mongolia. If there was a bright side, it was that I'd put off buying my ticket until June 1, so at least I hadn't wasted any money on airfare to Paris and a train ticket to Strasbourg to meet my absentee girlfriend, off sightseeing in Asia. Something about my situation seemed familiar...and then I remembered Ellie, my Chicago friend with the bladder infection and the red swollen pee-pee whose friends had stood her up in Paris, left her alone and walking around the streets of Gay Paree like a common streetwalker. Was I that pathetic? Apparently so.

Trying to read between the lines of Chantal's letter and decipher her intentions occupied me for days. Did she want to end our relationship altogether? Not exactly, I decided. After all, she had invited me to accompany her to India. Still, the invitation seemed like an afterthought tossed in at the very end in order to sweeten the bitter pill of rejection, see you later, pal, don't call me, I'll call you. The fact that she'd rather go on a tour of impoverished Asia with a group of strangers than spend a hot, steamy summer with me lying half-naked on the beaches of Greece said it all: she'd had a change of heart. Clearly, her passion had cooled. Eventually I came to the depressing conclusion that she was less than enthusiastic about our future prospects. In truth, I had seen this coming since Chantal's visit at Christmas. I just didn't want to acknowledge our troubles openly.

Great, so where did that leave me? Here it was, almost summertime and the living was easy, but suddenly I had nowhere to go and nobody to go with. For days I kept Chantal's letter secret, too embarrassed to tell my friends that I 'd been jilted and my summer plans dashed, until last night when I finally fessed up to Dennis, Vicki and Susie. I figured I might as well break the news now, since it had to come out sooner or later. I didn't want to wait until classes ended and summer break officially started only to have one of them ask, "By the way, aren't you supposed to be in Europe?"

The four of us were sitting in the living room watching television coverage of the U.S. Senate Select Committee's hearings on Watergate, as we had all week long. Events were unfolding rapidly now, all the lies and treachery coming out into the light of day. So far this week Watergate conspirator James McCord had testified before the committee that a former White House aide had offered him executive clemency in return for his silence. Meanwhile, Archibald Cox had been named as special Watergate prosecutor. Then yesterday Nixon released a statement on Watergate in which he admitted to limiting the investigation into the matter because of "national security" reasons (the same old smokescreen used by all political scoundrels in Washington when they're caught red-handed engaging in illegal activity). But instead of issuing a *mea culpa*, Tricky Dick blamed his over-zealous aides who he said had exceeded his instructions in attempting a cover-up of White House involvement in the break-in of Democratic National Headquarters in the Watergate Hotel.

"By the way, I have some news," I announced during a commercial break, then hesitated when I saw them all turn to stare at me, expecting some juicy gossip concerning Heather or one of the art department babes that Joe and Andy occasionally brought up to our apartment for a hot tryst. "My plan to spend the summer in Greece has changed. Turns out Chantal decided to go to India instead, with or without me."

Dennis registered first. "India? Shit! Why India?"

Vicki and Susie nodded their agreement. Shit!

"Easy come, easy go," Vicki said after a moment's reflection. She adjusted her glasses and brushed her long black hair out of her eyes. "I mean, you picked her up in a train station, right?"

"You picked her up in a train station?" Susie was incredulous. "What did you expect?"

"Actually, she picked me up," I said. "She gave me her name and address. It was her country. I was just a helpless tourist."

"Oh boy, now you've lost your cachet," Vicki said. "Without a French girlfriend not even Heather will sleep with you. I know I won't. You might have had a chance to get in my pants before, but not now, buddy boy."

"You slept with Heather! That bimbo? You ass!" Susie scolded me.

"Oh, don't flatter him, who hasn't slept with Heather? Except Dennis," Vicki added.

Someone had to defend sweet Heather, so I said, "Who says she's a bimbo. That depends on how you define bimbo." Not much of a defense, in retrospect.

Dennis looked perplexed. "So...are you planning to go to India with Chantal?"

"Fuck no! I have no interest in going to India. I'd rather slit my fucking wrists!" A slight exaggeration, but they got the point.

"So what are you going to do this summer?" Dennis asked.

I shrugged.

Dennis scrunched up his forehead and pondered my situation. As the problem solver among us, Dennis always tried to think things through to their logical conclusion. He was Mr. Rational, the Ann Landers of 1631 F, providing sound advice and useful suggestions to his hopelessly troubled friends, many of whom had fucked up their lives beyond repair. "I suppose you could work, try to save some money for next year or this fall, whenever you can connect with Chantal," he said finally.

Vicki had a different idea, delivered with the usual dose of sarcasm. "Or...you could take some classes and finish graduate school, like you're always saying you will. Actually finish something for once in your life!"

Though practical, and certainly productive, neither of those ideas excited me. It was summer we were talking about here. Summer!

"Or you could visit Alan in Santa Fe," Susie said suddenly, out of the blue. "You could borrow my roommate's car–I'm sure she wouldn't mind. Yeah, and I would even go with you."

The thought of a quick trip to Santa Fe had crossed my mind. Since returning to New Mexico in January, Alan had been writing letters almost weekly, describing the joys of living in the sunny Southwest. He bragged about Santa Fe's magical charm, its adobe architecture and enclosed courtyards, with the Sangre de Cristo Mountains North and East of the city. New Mexico had always been home to a vibrant arts community, attracting the likes of D.H. Lawrence, Willa Cather, and Georgia O'Keeffe, who still lived in her Abiquiu home overlooking the desert landscape she'd spent most of her life painting. Art, literature, and the sunny Southwest, what else did I need?

More to the point, as far as Alan was concerned, was that Taos County in northern New Mexico had become the freak capital of America, thanks in part to Dennis Hopper who'd come to Taos in 1969 while filming *Easy Rider*. By 1970, when Hopper and friends moved to Taos and bought the historic Mabel Dodge Luhan house not far from Taos Pueblo, some 3,000 freaks had congregated in and around Taos, living separately or in large communes like New Buffalo, the commune featured in *Easy Rider*. Other communes had names like Morning Star East, Reality, and Magic Tortoise. You could almost tell what the freaks were smoking by reading the names of their groups.

"Christ, Wilson, you wouldn't believe what's happening here!" Alan had written just last week. "Rumor has it that Hopper and his friends from L.A. are buying 100,000 acres of land between Taos and Arroyo Hondo.

They're planning to invite all the freaks in America to move there and pitch teepees and grow vegetables and get back to nature! Can you see it, row after row of teepees, with brothers and sisters working the land and tending the crops, all in the name of communal living and free love, man! It's going to be the Free Freak Nation, the United States of Freakdom, man! And Dennis Hopper will be the first president, like George fucking Washington!"

He'd ended his letter with a short, cryptic note: P.S. "I'm living in a yurt I built just south of Santa Fe. I'll send directions. Bring cold beer and food."

I considered for a few brief moments. What did I have to lose? I mean, it wasn't as though I had a lot of other options or invitations. My onetime girlfriend was off to Asia without me. I had nothing else to look forward to, other than work or graduate school, neither of which struck me as a proper way to spend a summer. So why not the Free Freak Nation, Dennis Hopper president?

"That's not a bad idea, Susie." I thought about it a bit more. "Okay, I'll do it, but only on one condition."

"Here it comes," Vicki said. "He'll want you to sleep with him, but don't do it, he's lost his cachet. Get used to it, Wilson. No more sex for you until you get another French girlfriend."

Susie rolled her eyes. "One condition? Let me guess."

"Yep...that you leave your cards at home."

Dennis laughed. "No sex and no Bridge. That'll make for a great summer.

Santa Fe. August 30, 1973

"I thought Alan lived in Santa Fe," Susie complained.

"South of Santa Fe. In a yurt."

"What's a yurt?"

We were driving a new VW bug, thanks to Susie's roommate, along Highway 14 through a coal mining railroad ghost town called Madrid.

Instead of majestic adobes and enclosed courtyards, we passed by huge mounds of black coal and gray, dilapidated buildings, most of them either missing timber or totally collapsed. It looked more like Appalachia, circa 1930, than his description of the sunny Southwest. It was hard to imagine a writer's colony out here. Alan had given me precise directions and mileage markers to the ten-acre parcel he'd supposedly purchased, legally or illegally he wasn't sure which, from a notorious local land swindler and on which he'd built, with a little help from some of his freak friends, his palatial homestead, the so-called yurt.

So now, one year ago to the day that I flew from Paris to Chicago, and on the same day the White House announced that Nixon would appeal Judge John J. Sirica's order to hand over the infamous White House tapes, Susie and I found ourselves headed south out of Madrid into a more inviting landscape of triangular hills dotted with Piñon and chamisa. We were looking for a dog-leg to the right, a turn-off that would take us up a small hill to a gated cattle pasture. Somewhere on the other side of the gate at the end of the yellow brick road, Alan the wizard and his yurt awaited our arrival. We'd come bearing gifts of cold beer and food, as directed. But we brought with us no deck of playing cards. As promised, Susie had left her cards at home.

"What the fuck is a yurt?" Susie asked again.

""I think it's some kind of round hut, like they build in Outer Mongolia or someplace like that. I don't know. We'll find out soon enough."

Susie pointed up ahead to a narrow, nearly invisible gravel road that jutted off to the right. I made the sharp turn and rolled to a stop in front of a metal gate, which had a cattle guard underneath. Not bothering to wait for me, Susie jumped out of the VW and climbed up on the gate. "Look at that. He lives in a cow pasture!"

Sure enough, when I joined her at the gate, I saw several head of cattle gathered at a cow tank about 50 yards beyond the gate. Above them the blades of a windmill churned slowly in the breeze, pumping water out of the dry desert ground into the tank. Otherwise I saw absolutely nothing except piñon and juniper trees, prickly pear and yucca cactus, and chamisa bushes abloom in bright yellow. Talk about desolate, even the gravel road seemed to disappear on the other side of the gate, becoming a couple of ruts in the dirt that faded to dust halfway to the water tank. It was so hot that heat waves rippled my field of vision, turning the landscape into an hallucinogenic maze of squiggly lines and splotches of color, mostly smoky shades of green, gray, and brown. Just gazing off in the distance made you feel like you were on an acid trip.

Susie went back to the driver's side of the VW and honked the horn a few times, then a few more times for good measure. At first the only movement I saw was that of the cows scattering, moving away from the water tank. Then from somewhere unseen beyond the trees came a blood-curdling scream: "Wilsooooonnnnn!" A few moments later we saw Alan, or what we assumed was Alan, walking slowly down the road into view. He seemed to materialize out of the rippling heat waves like a vision, a Biblical vision, Jesus walking on water or God appearing to Moses in the desert. His hair and beard were even longer and shaggier than before, and he walked with a giant walking stick (a serpent he'd turned to wood?). Even though it must have been 90 plus degrees, he wore the same clothes he always wore: jeans, flannel shirt, and his impossibly large, impregnable hiking books laced with red rope.

"Wilson...you made it. I can't believe you're here." He stopped when he spotted Susie lurking behind the VW.

"Don't worry, I left my cards at home," Susie said.

"Well, in that case..." Alan opened the gate and gave us both a bear hug. He smelled like he hadn't taken a shower since we'd last seen him in January.

He and Susie led the way walking, while I followed along behind in the VW. I'd been right about the road disappearing halfway to the water tank, but Alan knew the way like the back of his hand. He veered off to the right, through a tangle of piñon trees, ending up in a flat, open meadow. There, in the center of the open area, stood the mighty yurt, a crude round structure built from rough-cut pine. About the same size as a large teepee, it had a sloped, pointed roof covered with tarpaper. A flimsy outhouse had been dug off to the side, separated from the yurt by a good fifty feet.

Alan opened his arms wide, as though he were about to part the desert. "Welcome to my house. We built it ourselves this summer. Come on inside, but watch your heads."

Susie and author at Alan's yurt, Madrid, New Mexico, 1973 (courtesy of Alan Boye).

Susie and I ducked as we stepped inside and up onto the raised wooden floor of the yurt. As we walked around, we could hear rodents and rattlesnakes rustling around underneath the floorboards, looking for food scraps or people to bite and/or infect with bubonic plague. Around the inner circumference Alan had built benches, which could be used for sitting or sleeping. He had more benches and storage areas in the center, built around the central post, which anchored the post-and-beam construction and the radial rafters overhead. The entire structure, Alan pointed out, was held together by a tension band that encircled the outside, holding the vertical side boards in place much as a rubber band would hold a bunch of wooden matches together, standing upright. There was no electricity, no running water, and no ventilation other than the curtained door and a couple of cubbyhole windows that didn't provide much light or fresh air. If it was 90 degrees outside, it was easily 100 degrees inside with the desert sun beating down mercilessly on the black roof. Even though Susie and I were both wearing shorts and sandals, the inside of the yurt felt as hot as a sweat lodge.

The author at Alan's yurt, Madrid, New Mexico, 1973 (courtesy of Alan Boye).

"If I have to sleep in here tonight, I'm going to have to get really drunk," Susie said. "Do you hear me? Really drunk!"

"Not a problem," Alan said, bringing out a half gallon of cheap bourbon. In addition to the bourbon, Alan had a five-gallon plastic container filled with water from the cow tank and a fairly robust stash of pot. Other than those nutritious items, high on the food pyramid, he had no food or drink or any way of keeping anything cold if he had something to keep cold.

"No, I mean drunk as in lots of cold beer, more cold beer than we brought with us," Susie said.

"Still no problem. We'll just drive into Santa Fe."

Which, as it turned out, was how Alan managed to survive living outside civilization in his yurt. His girlfriend, Brenda, came by every other day or so to take him into town and buy him lunch or dinner. They usually stopped at a liquor store on their way back to the yurt. So much for the myth of self-sufficiency.

Before leaving for Santa Fe, Alan wanted to show us around his land, so he grabbed his walking stick and took us on a tour of his ten acres, every acre looking exactly the same as the other nine. The view, however, was nothing short of spectacular. Through the thin mountain air we could see great distances with the clarity that only the high desert provides. To the North we saw Santa Fe and the Sangre de Cristo Mountains. To the west we saw Los Alamos, high in the Jemez Mountains, where the world's first nuclear bombs had been built in the 1940s.

By the time we finished the tour, Susie and I were as hot, sweaty, and nearly as smelly as Alan. The time had come for cold beer and food, so the three of us drank what we had on hand and then piled into the VW bug and drove into Santa Fe. We stopped at a dark but cool biker's joint on Cerrillos Road called Blues and Barbecue. Inside, the place looked like a big barn, with rows of tables in front and a stage in the rear, where local bands covered the latest rock and country hits. Some unknown foursome, with a lead singer who looked like an aging hippie version of Grace Slick, was singing "Who'll Stop the Rain" as we walked in and found an empty table up front.

A platter of ribs and two pitchers of beer later, feeling revived, we piled back into the VW and took a quick tour of Santa Fe. Alan sat in the rear seat and served as tour guide, directing us first to the Plaza downtown, which had been the heart of the city at least since the winter of 1609–1610, when the newly appointed governor of the Spanish province of New Mexico, Pedro de Peralta, founded *La Villa Real de la Santa Fe de San Francisco de Asís*, or the Royal City of the Holy Faith of Saint Francis of Assisi, as the capitol of the new province. Part of the original government buildings, or *Casas Reales*, could still be seen in the current Palace of the Governors, the building on the North side of the Plaza. From there we walked over to San Miguel Chapel, supposedly the oldest church in America, dating from the early 1600s, maybe as early as 1605. Alan pointed out that if Santa Fe wasn't the oldest city in the U.S. ("Fuck Saint Augustine, Florida!") then at least it was the oldest state capitol in America. After his tour we ended up at the bar at the La Fonda Hotel ("Best damn hotel in Santa Fe!") where we enjoyed more beers and baskets of chips and at closing time one more round of beers for the road.

Trying to walk back to the VW, Susie said, "Oh fuck! I'm gonna have a killer hangover tomorrow. You asses, I blame you!"

"You were the one who wanted cold beer," I pointed out.

She waved at Alan. "That's because he lives in a fucking cow pasture!"

"Hey–at least it's my own land. I own it, man. It's mine."

"I thought freaks were opposed to private property. Ever hear of Karl Marx?"

"Come on, you two, stop fighting," I said. "We're not even playing Bridge."

"He's too stupid to play Bridge!"

"Don't start," Alan said.

"Fuck you both," Susie said. "You know what...I'm leaving, because I'm a modern girl and I need my luxuries. I'm gonna check into La Fonda tonight, and then tomorrow morning I'm gonna drive home by myself. It's my roommate's car. You two assholes can walk back to the yurt and go fuck yourselves!"

With that, Susie turned and headed back toward La Fonda. She made it as far as the first curb before tripping and falling flat on the sidewalk. Alan and I managed to get her back to the car by half carrying, half dragging her. She cursed like a truck driver and fought us every step of the way, but as soon as we hit the highway she curled up on the back seat and fell sound asleep.

"How do you put up with it, Wilson?" Alan wanted to know, raising his voice above the sound of Susie snoring behind us.

"It's the two of you. I get along fine with her...except maybe when we're playing Bridge."

By the time we made it back to the yurt it was after two a.m. Exhausted, we still faced the problem of what to do with Susie. Should we let her sleep in the VW with the windows open for fresh air, or should we try to move her into the yurt. Unfortunately, we decided on the latter course of action, a big mistake. As we should have guessed, Susie woke up screaming when we attempted to pull her out of the back seat. In the melee that followed, we lost our grip and dropped her momentarily, just long enough for her to smack her head on the floorboard. "Let go of me, you big apes!"

"Sorry. Just trying to help," I said.

While Alan lit a kerosene lantern inside the yurt and arranged sleeping bags, Susie stumbled off to the outhouse. I took my time before going inside, where the temperature had cooled to a chilly 90 or 95 degrees.

Suddenly we heard a yelp, and then a full-fledge scream. "Help! Get me out of this outhouse! I'm falling in!"

Alan rushed to help Susie. I could hear the two of them arguing off in the darkness, but I didn't offer to intervene. Let the two of them come to a truce or kill each other in the process. I was too tired to care.

Eventually Susie came back to the yurt mumbling, "Can't even pee out here..."

I heard her collapse on top of her sleeping bag, still cursing, and then Alan saying, "I'm blowing out the lantern, Wilson."

"Okay, I'm coming."

Somehow, in some inexplicable way, I felt indescribably happy to be outside by myself, away from my friends, the kind of absolute peace and contentment I hadn't felt in months.

Somewhere in the distance I heard the lonesome sound of coyotes wailing. Overhead, a million stars twinkled in the night sky. I'd never seen so many stars so clearly. The nearest town, Santa Fe, was at least ten miles away. While I watched, the stars seemed to move faster and faster, all of them traveling away from me at the speed of light, driven further into empty space by Einstein's mysterious anti-gravity force, his explanation for the ever-expanding, ever-accelerating universe.

Every so often I heard Susie and Alan bickering inside the yurt. "Get offa me, you fucker!" Susie would yell.

"Shut up! I'm just trying to help you into the sleeping bag!"

Minutes passed. I never moved. I simply sat there watching the universe fly apart in fragments, strangely comforted by this magnificent display of cosmic dispersion.

The dry desert air and the scent of sage and piñon reminded me of somewhere I'd been not so long ago. Yugoslavia.

S trasbourg. Feb. 22, 1974

   James,

   J'ai bein reçu ta letter. Tu peux bien sûr passer à Strasbourg me render visite. J'espère que tu vas bien et t'evoie toutes mes amities.

   —Chantal

L incoln. July 15, 1974

   A cruel "Building Condemned" sign had appeared on the front door of our building earlier in the week. What had been inevitable for years finally had come to pass: the wrecking ball was on its way to demolish our building. For me it marked the end of an era, the end of my life at 1631 F. Dennis and I had to be out of the apartment by September 1, the thought of which expedited our decisions and planning for the future. We were all dispersing, Dennis off to medical school, Vicki off to law school, and me off to Santa Fe with Susie to start a new life without Chantal.

Susie had decided to accompany me to Santa Fe. She'd made her peace with Alan thanks to the good graces and mediation of Brenda, Alan's girlfriend, who'd taken him in after he'd grown tired of living at the yurt with only rattlesnakes, rodents, and cows for company. While Dennis and I packed up our apartment, Susie was at home doing the same. I was supposed to pick her up first thing in the morning on my way out of town in my new car: a 1961 Chevy Impala with 70,000 miles and a new set of used tires. The car was my graduation gift to myself after finally finishing the M.A. program I'd been enrolled in for more years than I cared to remember. I'd taken care of all my unfinished business and was ready to move on with my life.

Originally we planned on throwing a going away/demolition party but decided against it when moving proved to be so exhausting. Our living room and hallway were filled with stacks of books and household items, which we'd divided up evenly, more or less. Never very neat, we'd stopped cleaning altogether after the Building Condemned sign appeared on our door, so now the apartment was littered with garbage and empty beer bottles. We were told that the building and everything inside it, including furniture, would be pulverized by the wrecking ball and then carted away to the city dump. Which was fine, since none of us wanted the hand-me-down furniture anyway. In response, someone had thrown a white sheet over the piano and then painted a target on the sheet with bright red paint that had dripped down onto the floor and pooled like blood. Living in the apartment now was like living inside a dumpster.

Joe and Faye had volunteered to come over to help, but by help they meant sitting on the living room sofa and giving advice on what items to keep and what to throw away, except that pretty much everything I showed them elicited the same response: "Throw that shit away! Toss it! Why would you want to keep that?" Dennis, Vicki, and I would work for about an hour, under the supervision of Joe and Faye, and then take a two-hour break to drink beer and light up a number or two, courtesy of Joe. After working all day, we had little to show for our labor except a few piles of crap to be saved, a sea of empty beer bottles, and an ashtray full of roaches.

"At this rate, you'll never be able to finish by tomorrow morning," Faye said, sitting comfortably on the sofa.

"Man, I think you might be better off to leave it all for the wrecking ball. Fuck it!" Joe added.

I was beginning to agree with them when I came across Chantal's letters and postcards in my bedroom. "I can't throw these away." I showed them the letters.

"Whatever," Joe said.

Faye wasn't nearly as circumspect. "As if she'll keep yours!"

While we argued about Chantal's correspondence, Dennis and Vicki joined us in the living room. Dennis brought more beers, which he passed around and then took a seat on the piano bench next to Vicki. "Time for a break. Haven't we worked for nearly an hour?"

Joe nodded. "Absolutely. This is exhausting."

Just then we heard a knock on the door at the bottom of the stairway, which was unusual because none of our friends ever bothered to knock. They just walked right up the stairs or climbed the fire escape. At first we thought it was a stranger, but then we recognized a short blond guy with glasses who we'd seen lately hanging around with Heather downstairs. He was a creative writing student at the university whose name was Jeremy, but Heather pronounced it JUR-a-me, why I don't know, maybe because he was at least a foot shorter than Heather. When standing side by side, his nose came up to her nipples, which made them look ridiculous as a couple, even if they were both blond-haired and fair-skinned Nordic types. When together, the two of them looked like they should be in a poster for the Master Race.

"Sorry, he didn't know he wasn't supposed to knock," Heather said, flashing Jeremy a frown.

"No need to knock," I said. "Any friend of Heather's is a friend of ours."

"Speak for yourself," Vicki said.

Jeremy walked stiffly into the living room, which is when we noticed the notebook in his hand and gave a collective groan. Jeremy had come to do one of his readings. As an undergraduate creative writing major at the university, a self-proclaimed poet of the Everyday, whatever that meant, he had the irritating habit of appearing uninvited at public events or at the homes of friends in moments of great personal change or crisis with a new poem he'd penned just for the occasion. He was like the Angel of Death, except perhaps a little less somber, popping up unexpectedly to take you away to the everlasting hell of undergraduate creative writing class.

While we sat frozen in place, helpless to stop what was about to go down, Jeremy positioned himself in the corner of the apartment, beside the open fire escape window. He cleared his throat. "This poem is entitled 'Demolition.' I wrote it in honor of this sad occasion, the death of 1631 F." He cleared his throat again and then put on his most serious poetry face. When he began reading, he spoke in a deep un-Jeremy-like voice as though his body had been taken over by an unseen ventriloquist using him as a dummy to mouth the words that followed: "I saw the best minds of my generation stoned out of their minds, high on acid, vomiting into the vortex of history."

"How original!" Vicki said. "Let me guess, the title is 'Woof' or maybe 'Bark'."

Joe stopped mid-toke. "Wait, did he say 'vomiting into the vortex of history'?"

"I'm afraid he did," Faye said. "You weren't hallucinating. This time."

"Stop! No More! You're bumming us out!" Dennis said, taking charge as he usually did in tricky, uncomfortable situations. "I mean, I don't want to hurt your feelings, but shut the fuck up!"

Instantly Jeremy got this sour, pained look on his face, as though he'd been betrayed by his best friends. "Yeah...it's a work in progress."

Joe sauntered over to Jeremy and gave his shoulder a friendly squeeze. "Keep working on it, kid. But take out that line about vomiting into the vortex. That could do some serious psychological damage to your readers."

On his way back to the sofa, Joe gawked at Heather's luscious cleavage a bit too conspicuously. Like Dennis, Joe had the hots for Heather big time. He'd tried for years to get her into bed, but Heather had taken an instant disliking to *le philosophe de la chatte* and refused to give him the time of day. She shot him a dirty look as he walked past, intentionally brushing up against her tits. "Oops...sorry...ha, ha, ha...my bad."

After witnessing the whole blatant incident from across the room, Faye gave Joe the finger and got up to leave. She slammed the door at the bottom of the stairway.

Now that Jeremy had ruined our break, we went back to work packing. Jeremy lingered for a few more minutes until he realized no one was paying any attention to him, at which point he tucked his notebook under his arm with great solemnity and shuffled off toward the stairway, following Faye out of the apartment.

A few minutes later Joe accosted me in my bedroom, where I was packing the last of my personal affairs. "Hey, man, are you fucking Heather?" He passed me the joint he'd just lit as though it were truth serum. "Fess up, James."

"I'll take the Fifth on that—"

"I knew it! You motherfucker! How'd you ever get into that?"

"Simple. She likes the sensitive type," I said, exhaling.

"What? You mean I'm not sensitive?"

I laughed. "Joe, you're a lot of things, but sensitive isn't one of them."

He shook his head sadly. "What a trip. She prefers you to me because you're a pussy, I mean because you're the sensitive type. I must be losing my touch."

"Not you. You're still *le philosophe de la chatte*, like Chantal said."

"I don't think so, I've lost the title," he said. Then he took back his joint and sucked on what was left of it before wandering off into the living room.

I worked for another hour or so before deciding that Joe and Faye were right. Let the wrecking ball have most of the crap. I packed my books, my clothes, and the minimum amount of household items required to start up an apartment in Santa Fe. Whatever I took, I had to leave room in the car for Susie's stuff, however much crap she decided to bring, or endure her wrath all the way to Santa Fe. So after I finished dragging boxes downstairs and stuffing them in my trusty '61 Impala, I called it quits and retreated to the kitchen to see what I could find for dinner. As usual, our cupboards were bare and the refrigerator smelled rancid, so I made a mental list of groceries to buy at the local IGA.

While I pondered dinner, I heard the unmistakable sound of Heather's sandals shuffling up the stairs. My heart skipped a beat. I half-wished she would go back down instead of continuing on into the kitchen. I had no will power when it came to Heather, none whatsoever. She was impossible for me to resist. Oh, I'd tried to refuse her charms, but the flesh was weak and getting weaker now that Chantal was out of the picture. My only defense was to hide like a coward, hoping to go unnoticed. As I held my breath, to no avail, Heather poked her blond head around the corner and said, "There you are. I've been looking for you."

"Yep, here I am."

Heather looked absolutely radiant today, with a tight flower print skirt and a skimpy turquoise top. I imagined the exquisite pleasure of removing her skirt and top and what was underneath, if anything. She slithered up to me, rubbing her lascivious breasts against my chest and kissing me with an open mouth. Then, grabbing my ass with both hands, she pulled me hard into her hips. "I have a going away present for you."

I was confused. "What about your boyfriend?"

"He's not my boyfriend. He just follows me around. He gets lost when I tell him to...and I just told him to get lost for the rest of the day. So why don't you come down, say about ten o'clock."

"Okay, I'll come."

"Yes, you will," she said, breaking into a big smile.

With that Heather turned and sashayed out of the kitchen. I watched fondly as her hips swayed to a magical bossa nova beat that only Heather seemed to hear. I would miss Heather–playful, unpredictable, ebullient Heather. You could wander the world and never find brownies as good as Heather's. I enjoyed every moment I spent with her...and yet there was always something missing between us...a deeper bond that would hold us together. Something more than sex.

As for Chantal and I, our relationship never really ended. It simply faded away over the years, from visits to letters to postcards and finally to silence. The last communication I had from her, a short postcard in response to my last letter to her, invited me to stop by and visit should I ever be passing through Strasbourg. Not exactly the kind of relationship I had envisioned back in Yugoslavia. In the end the two of us were bodies in motion moving in opposite directions, in different careers and on different continents, separated by time and space and all the usual and ordinary things that can come between even the most compatible of people.

It was time to move on.

S anta Fe. August 9, 1974

"I have never been a quitter," Richard Nixon said, jowls flapping, as he addressed the American people and announced his resignation as president effective at noon today. His allies on Capitol Hill had told him there were more than enough votes in the House of Representatives to impeach him and more than enough votes in the Senate to convict him. As a consequence his only option was to eat his words, become a quitter, and get out of town fast before the House could start the process.

So here we were, shortly after ten a.m. Mountain Standard Time, drinking beer and cheering the overhead television at the Washington Street Deli, directly across the street from the Museum of New Mexico's Historical Library. Alan, Susie and I were sitting at a table among the dozens of other people who packed the small delicatessen, with another dozen or so spilling out the door to the patio tables outside. Most everyone at the Deli had spent their entire youth hating Nixon's guts and doing everything possible to subvert his presidency and his war in Vietnam, so this was a day like no other, a day for celebration. After Nixon relinquished power and turned over the black box to his stooge and soon-to-be pardoner Gerald Ford, he and his family climbed aboard a military helicopter to be whisked away to Andrews Air Force Base in Maryland. From there the Nixons would be flown by Air Force One back to California in disgrace, one final waste of taxpayer money.

When Tricky Dick waved his last goodbye and the helicopter began to lift off above the White House lawn, the Deli crowd responded with a rousing cheer, accompanied by catcalls and obscene gestures. Most of us never thought this day would ever happen, because Nixon had been so slippery for so long. For him to get caught and go out like a common criminal was too sweet for words. We were positively giddy with victory, naively believing that the forces of Good had triumphed once and for all over the forces of Evil. Why not admit it, we were convinced that history had been righted, that peace and justice would now prevail at home and abroad, that the Age of Aquarius would finally be realized. In other words, we were a bunch of damned fools.

"Good riddance motherfucker!" someone in the crowd shouted as the helicopter disappeared into the wild blue yonder.

As soon as the live telecast ended, the Deli crowd quieted down and began to disperse.

"Well, unlike you guys, I have to go back to work," Alan announced, finishing his beer and leaving some money on the table. He had found a job at the Santa Fe Public Library so as not to rely on his girlfriend Brenda for support. He worked first as the Bookmobile driver and later as the nominal head of the newly formed audio-visual department.

Susie loved to tease Alan, especially when, like today, she was in a festive mood. "Too bad, I plan to sit here all morning drinking beer and fucking off, but then I don't have to make payments on ten acres of cow pasture and a wooden shack, do I, sucker!"

Alan winced.

"Or should I say ten illegally-purchased acres of cow pasture!"

"I'm not listening," Alan said, turning away and clomping through the crowd in his Mount Everest hiking boots.

I took a big gulp and asked, "Do you ever think that maybe you're too hard on Alan?"

"Who's hard on him? What are you talking about?"

"Never mind." I held up my hand in a gesture of peace. Susie was not someone you wanted to get into an argument with.

Susie and I were temporarily renting a small adobe on Jose Street, surrounded by people who claimed to be writers and artists, many of them potters who spent the better part of every day hunched over a potter's wheel or firing up their kiln. We were all young, artistically inclined, and looking to find our way in the world. Subsequently, I would live in a house on Galisteo Street, a guest house in Tesuque, an apartment on East Palace Avenue, and one summer I earned my counterculture bonafides by living in a teepee on Nine Mile Road.

Alan at his writing desk in our house
on Galisteo Street, Santa Fe, New Mexico, 1975

(photograph by author).

But it was on Jose Street that I was properly introduced to Santa Fe. I was told by more than one of my neighbors that my aura was sorely in need of balancing. What that meant I had no idea, since I had never heard of aura balancing before coming to Santa Fe. I assumed what they meant, what they were trying to tell me however obliquely, was that my personality was out of whack, that I had some issues to deal with. What else was new? In the meantime I'd found a part-time job at a weekly newspaper doing everything from composition to photography to feature writing. Later I began freelancing for the daily newspaper.

The La Fonda Hotel, Santa Fe, New Mexico, 2018 (photograph by author).

Though I lived and worked in Santa Fe, I spent almost as much time exploring New Mexico, hiking in the national forests and camping in the mysterious Chaco Canyon, where a thousand years earlier the Ancestral Puebloans had built a metropolis with roads, dams, irrigation, and Great Houses of magnificent stone. The Pax Chaco had lasted from 860 to about 1060 AD, during which the Chacoans traded with other Indigenous cultures as far away as California, Mexico and Central America.

Chaco Canyon, Pueblo Bonito from North Mesa, 2016 (photograph by author).

I realized early on that for me the Outdoor Life had replaced my traveling, just as traveling had replaced my anti-war activities back in the early seventies. My explorations enabled me to pursue my passion for photography, shooting black and white film at first and then mostly color when the digital age arrived. My treks, armed with camera and tripod, took me on long camping trips in the Pecos, the Jemez, the Carson, and along the Chama River.

Who had time to work when there was so much to discover? My research took me first to Taos, the freak capitol of America, where I was a frequent visitor to Arroyo Hondo. I was equally interested in the Mabel Dodge Luhan house, next to Taos Pueblo, where you could feel the spirits of those who had lived and visited there. Mabel Dodge bought the house in 1918 and moved her New York salon from Greenwich Village to Taos, where she held court for the leading artists and free thinkers of the Progressive Era, including writers such as D.H. Lawrence, Willa Cather, and Aldous Huxley; artists such as Georgia O'Keeffe, Ansel Adams, and Alfred Stieglitz; and intellectuals such as John Reed, Margaret Sanger, and Carl Jung. When Mabel married Tony Luhan from the Taos Pueblo, their union was referred to as a marriage of West and East, western culture and eastern philosophy.

The Mabel Dodge Luhan House, Taos, New Mexico, 2018 (photograph by author).

Mabel played a central role in bringing D.H. Lawrence and his wife Frieda to Taos in 1924. Mabel gave Frieda a ranch on Lobo Mountain near San Cristobal, about 20 miles northwest of Taos, which became the Lawrence's summer home for two years and, after Lawrence's death in 1930, the home of Frieda until her death in 1956. Lawrence's ashes were supposedly mixed with the concrete used to build the Lawrence Memorial on the ranch property, which Frieda bequeathed to the University of New Mexico at the time of her death.

Taos Pueblo, North House, 1975 (photograph by author).

Like the Mabel Dodge Luhan house, the Lawrence Ranch was adopted by the 1970s counterculture that descended on Taos before and after the arrival of Dennis Hopper, who bought the Luhan house in March 1970 and lived there on and off until January 1978. Hopper brought with him artists, radicals, and freaks from both Los Angeles and New York. If you drove up to the Luhan house on any given day in the mid 1970s, you might expect to encounter rock stars, famous actors and directors, the guiding lights of pop culture. The house was a free-for-all, a non-stop "happening." Sometimes when you walked in you had no idea who was living there or who was visiting invited or uninvited. Everyone was always stoned. Some people claimed to see the angry ghosts of Mabel and Tony who were not happy about what was currently going down in their house.

On one evening not long after my arrival in Santa Fe I was sitting out on the veranda of the sprawling Luhan house when a young couple, two freaks in black leather, rode up on a Harley. The guy wandered off somewhere toward the rear of the house, from where you could see Taos Pueblo land. Unconcerned with her companion, the young woman walked unsteadily to the veranda and flashed me the peace sign. "Hey–man–is it, like, okay if we crash here tonight?"

I threw open my hands, not knowing what to say. "Uh...well, I..."

"Far out, man! Thanks!" She removed her helmet, revealing a pretty face and a shock of red hair that cascaded down her back. "We heard you were a real cool dude. We love your movies!"

Only after she stumbled into the house did it occur to me that she thought I was Dennis Hopper. It was that crazy.

Later that evening I saw her again in the kitchen, where she and at least a dozen other freaks were snacking on chips, brownies, and other munchies. As soon as she spotted me, she dropped her snacks and headed my way. Tossing her arms around my neck, she whispered: "Where's your bedroom?"

I looked around for the boyfriend who was nowhere to be seen.

I took her arm. "This way."

Down the dark hallway we found a small back bedroom with a single twin bed pushed up against the adobe wall and a lock on the door, all we needed. Though stoned, we were both feeling pretty sexy. She jumped on top of me as soon as we hit the bed, wet kisses and hands everywhere, moaning and calling me Dennis this, Dennis that. At the moment I didn't mind being an alias lover, all I wanted to do was get into her pants fast. That turned out to be a problem, because her leather pants were so tight that it took what seemed like ten minutes to get the snap unfastened and then, try as I might, I couldn't pull the skintight pants down over her luscious hips. As I struggled with the pants I suddenly realized my leather–clad lover had stopped moving, and before I had time to turn on a light to see what had happened, I heard her snoring on the bed, sound asleep.

Easy come, easy go.

I spent as much time at the D.H. Lawrence ranch as I did at the Mabel Dodge Luhan house, staying frequently in the cabins that the University of New Mexico maintained and rented, mostly to counterculture types who regarded Lawrence as a cult figure, a 1920s version of a freak. You could feel Lawrence's spirit most strongly around the "Lawrence Tree," a tall pine under which Lawrence used to write and which Georgia O'Keeffe made famous in her painting of the same name. More freaks dropped acid under the Lawrence Tree than any other spot on the ranch.

My other favorite Taos hangout was the Plaza, especially La Fonda de Taos, which also figured large in Taos mythology. La Fonda was a favorite meeting place of both the Luhan and Hopper sets as well as being the repository of D.H. Lawrence's "dirty" or "forbidden" paintings. The nine paintings, sold to the owner of the La Fonda after Lawrence's death, hardly raised an eyebrow in the 1970s and would be considered folksy and quaint by today's standards. Not so in 1929, when Scotland Yard confiscated the La Fonda nine and four other paintings from the Dorothy Warren Gallery of London and threatened to burn the paintings unless Lawrence promptly removed them from England, which he did. You have to remember that at the time Lawrence was considered something of a semi-pornographic artist because of the suppression of his novel, *Lady Chatterley's Lover* (1928) and the seizure of an earlier Lawrence novel, *The Rainbow* (1915).

Try as I might, I couldn't find anything remotely erotic, never mind pornographic, about the paintings. Images like "Flight back into Paradise," "Fauns and Nymphs," and even "Dance Sketch," which at least showed some bush, struck me as amateurish and just plain silly, the kind of folk art that could have been created by some freak out on a mesa near Arroyo Hondo with a pack of crayons in one hand and a joint in the other.

Taos held a special place in my heart, as did Abiquiu, where I spent an equal amount of time exploring. I always stopped first at the village, turning off on the steep road that took you up the mesa until, just as you reached the top, Georgia O'Keeffe's walled adobe compound came into view. A gracefully curving wall shrouded O'Keeffe's house, protecting the reclusive O'Keeffe, who by then only rarely ventured outside the walls of her creative fortress. The adobe architecture, with its gentle curves and rounded domes and its window and doorframes painted bright blue, reminded me of Greece or maybe Morocco. Susie was so taken with the village and its spectacular views that she and her on-again, off-again boyfriend, Tom, who'd made arrangements to join her at the end of summer, had rented the house closest to O'Keeffe's. Part of their daily routine would consist of a Georgia watch, waiting to get a glimpse of the fabled old woman dressed all in black.

The Chama River, near Abiquiu, 2016 (photograph by author).

After leaving the village, I would drive along the Chama River to Ghost Ranch, with its spectacular view of Pedernal, the flat-topped mountain that O'Keeffe made famous in her paintings. I loved hiking, alone or with friends from Santa Fe, high among the red rock canyons or down below among the pink and gray cliffs of the foothills. The sights and sounds and smells of the high desert, the blue sky and the pastel colors, everything about Abiquiu and Ghost Ranch reminded me of Yugoslavia, as I had been reminded that first night while sitting by myself outside Alan's yurt.

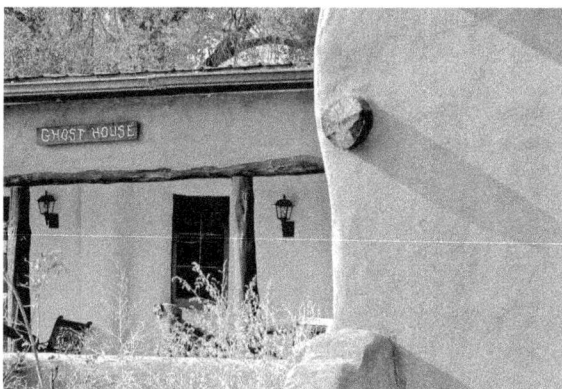

Ghost House at Ghost Ranch, 2015 (photograph by author).

I'll admit that when I first arrived in Santa Fe I thought of New Mexico as a consolation prize, a substitute for France, Greece, and all the places I might have gone with Chantal. But that changed rather quickly, because in Europe I had always been a tourist, rootless and constantly on the move. Even though I enjoyed my travels, I'd never felt at home in Pula or Strasbourg or Paris. I'd never felt at home anywhere until I moved to New Mexico. In Santa Fe I discovered the alternative culture I'd been seeking, an alternative to mainstream America, which had brought us Vietnam, the military-industrial complex, and the corrosive consumer capitalism that had eroded most of the values I held dear and driven me into exile in 1971.

It was in Santa Fe that I finally discovered an alternative way of being in the world, more attuned to the natural rhythms of earth and sky, paying homage to the Ancestral Puebloans who organized their society around an astronomical calendar in places like Chaco Canyon, Aztec, and Chimney Rock. I also discovered a different way of seeing the world, more focused on geometrical patters in the landscape and how, using light and color, I could abstract any image. Almost immediately I understood why artists and photographers and other pilgrims of life had been gathering in New Mexico for over a hundred years.

Like those earlier pilgrims, those of us in the 1970s counterculture came to Santa Fe searching for a different way of life, a more communal, connected life that rejected the American mythology that glorified individuality, isolated and mostly male. On the contrary, we valued the multi-cultural fabric of New Mexico, which deepened and enriched the texture of daily life. The mix of Native American, Hispanic, and Anglo cultures was the very thing that made New Mexico so special: it gave us a cross-cultural environment that allowed us to follow our own Life Roads.

I'm proud of what we created in Santa Fe, and I'm also proud to say that the counterculture is alive and well in New Mexico some fifty years later. In Taos, Santa Fe, Albuquerque, Silver City, and smaller communities across the state, community activists still struggle with issues of justice, identity, and equality. Native American and Hispanic rights organizations, beginning with such groups as the Black Mesa Defense Fund and La Raza, have shown how political these questions were then and remain today. Environmental justice, for example. Or basic equality: equal rights for all genders and ethnicities, including equal access to healthcare and to quality education. From food co-ops, health clinics, environmental and renewable energy groups, the cultural revolution engendered by the counterculture still shapes the social and political landscape of New Mexico.

Last year the New Mexico History Museum in Santa Fe sponsored "Voices of Counterculture in the Southwest," an exhibit that celebrated the counterculture's continuing contributions to New Mexico. Personally, I like to think I celebrate the counterculture every single day by the way I live my life. I owe all that to my decision to move to Santa Fe, because living in Santa Fe gave me the freedom to become myself. Whenever I would leave, even for short periods of time, I would long to be back in Santa Fe. I guess that's how I knew I'd found my home, my true city of refuge.

Not long after arriving in Santa Fe I sent Chantal a postcard with my new address, even though I never really expected a reply. I didn't get one. I could imagine her response: *"C'est fini."*

A lbuquerque. May 4, 1980

I thought of Chantal today after hearing the news that Marshal Tito had died from complications of a circulation disorder at a hospital in Ljubljana, Slovenia. He was 88.

My chance encounter with Tito remained a vivid memory. Nearly eight years had passed since I looked out that window in Pula, Yugoslavia, and saw the old man in the white suit and straw hat waving stiffly at the crowd from the back seat of his limousine. In my mind I saw the event unfold like a slow motion scene from a movie. The morning sunshine, the marching band, the cheering crowd, the flags and the flowers, I could picture every detail, as if I had been out on that windowsill only yesterday. I could still hear Chantal screaming for me to come back inside: "*Vite! Q'est ce que tu fais? Tu es completement fou!*"

My international *faux pas* might have been a disaster for me had it not been for Chantal's abilities as a translator and our landlord's skills as a negotiator. Without them, I might never have been allowed to leave Yugoslavia and return to Strasbourg with Chantal. Ultimately, I might never have made it back to the States, might never have moved to Santa Fe and then five years later to Albuquerque, where I entered a PhD program at the University of New Mexico.

That turned out to be my best decision ever, because it was at U.N.M. that I discovered the love of my life, a fellow graduate student, a dark-haired beauty who was as sophisticated as she was sexy. After a whirlwind romance, we came to the mutual conclusion that we could never be apart, not even for a single day, and so we were married on Leap Day, February 29, 1980.

Venice, March 2003

On my last trip to Venice I spent a long summer's day in St. Mark's Square. I toured St. Mark's Basilica and the Doge's Palace, paying my respects at the Bridge of Sighs to all the forlorn souls who had crossed over the bridge into eternity. That afternoon, drawn by memories, I found myself sitting alone on a bench at water's edge, gazing east across the Adriatic toward the city of Pula in the former Yugoslavia, to a time and place that no longer existed. For me, Venice and Pula were cities of memory, as ephemeral as the occasional wisps of clouds that dissolved into the steel blue sky, for it was here that I and my French companion had come many years before. I could almost imagine Chantal materializing out of the mob of tourists and sitting down beside me on the bench, even though Chantal and I had long since disappeared from each other's life. So, too, had Yugoslavia disappeared, having fragmented along ethnic lines back in the 1990s. Pula, where we had stayed, was now part of the independent republic of Croatia.

Partly it was the antique light in Venice that brought back so many memories– the fleeting, golden light of the Adriatic so conducive to memory and reflection. Watching the gondolas bob on the tide like brightly colored sprites dancing on water, I wondered if Chantal had ever returned to Pula, or maybe to Dubrovnik or somewhere else along the Dalmatian Coast, which in recent years had become a posh resort area. Maybe she'd gone back to Veruda Beach with a husband...or another companion. The thought of her going back with someone else filled me with conflicting emotions, but mostly I felt happy for her, hoping she, too, had found the love of her life.

Postscript

The author's post-freak townhome at La Luz del Oeste, 2018 (photograph by author).

Fifty years have passed since I stood with hundreds of other demonstrators in Grant Park across Michigan Avenue from the Conrad Hilton. We chanted and shouted anti-war slogans at the Illinois National Guard, which had blocked access to the Hilton with their jeeps and trucks. Earlier that day the Chicago Police had bloodied many of the young demonstrators with their nightsticks. Michigan Avenue was littered with signs and placards, shoes and items of clothing from the melee that had occurred earlier. Trying to save face, the Governor of Illinois had called in the National Guard after the brutality of the Chicago Police had been broadcast to the world by all the news media gathered in Chicago that week. The whole world watched what happened in Chicago, just as the whole world had watched what happened in Paris the preceding May.

Looking back, I see how young and naïve we were then. We thought our youthful energy and dedication could end the war, that we could bring about the kind of peaceful world our parents had fought and died for a mere twenty-five years before in World War II. Peace and love, equality and sexual freedom, and by all means the legalization of pot: that was our platform. It still is, more or less. What we didn't understand was that we were engaged in an ongoing culture war that had no beginning and would never end, no matter how many barricades we threw up or how many times we voted. Different generations, different religions, different races, different social-economic classes, different whatever: culture wars are inevitable. I should have realized this early on, because every time those of us on the Left demonstrated, those on the Right demonstrated against us. As in Paris in Mai '68, so it was in Chicago in August '68, with true believers on both sides of the barricades. *Soixante Huitards*, all of us.

Since then, of course, the culture wars have continued unabated. If anything, they've increased in intensity and vitriol, not to mention violence. Today the hot button issue happens to be immigration. Before that, abortion and the Second Amendment received most media attention here in the States. The Left wants legalized abortion, and the Right wants unrestricted gun rights. Toss in family values, racial equality, same-sex marriage, and income inequality, and you have the basics of Culture Wars for Dummies.

Politically, the struggle swings back and forth, toward one extreme and then the other: Nixon/Carter, Carter/Reagan, Bush/Cinton, and so on. What some of my more fervently radical friends don't recognize or won't admit is that, over time, the pendulum has always tacked back toward the center. I'll admit that Trump, our current racketeer president, is an outlier of sorts, the extreme rightward swing after Obama, but he comes from a long line of demagogues whose tactics we have seen before. Think Nixon, Wallace, Reagan, even George W Bush and his puppeteer, Dick Cheney.

Trump rode a wave of resentment and retaliation against the so-called elites into the White House. In addition, he was aided by his good friends the Russians, as well as the third and fourth party candidates and the nominal Democrats who stayed home or were too prissy to vote for Hillary. Apparent to just about every objective observer, Trump's candidacy was fueled by racism, misogyny, and xenophobia, all of which we've seen throughout the history of American politics. Though Trump was by and for the one percent, his storm troopers were the usual suspects: angry lower and middle class whites who blamed their declining social/economic status not on industrial decline or international capitalism but on the Other: blacks, Latinos, immigrants, the LGTB community, anyone and everyone who was different and therefore a threat to them. That is, they were the typical American mob, whipped up to a frenzy by Trump's hate speech: his insults, his race-bating, and the rest. They marched in step to Trump's promise to Make America Great Again by bringing back long-lost jobs and industries, by ending so-called special treatment for minorities, and by stopping immigration.

However, I think this too will pass. Trump and his Orwellian world of lies and propaganda will pass, and the pendulum will again swing leftward. Unlike some of my friends who think Trump is one of the Four Horsemen of the Apocalypse about to precipitate End Times, the destruction of America as we know it if not the planet itself, I have a slightly different take. I paraphrase the wise old figure of Claudius in *I Claudius*: let all the muck and the poison come out. This too will pass.

I can't speak for others, but personally I have no regrets. Looking back over the past 50 years there is little I would have left undone or done otherwise. I've been blessed with a happy marriage and a successful career as a college professor. I live in La Luz del Oeste, an environmentally friendly community on Albuquerque's West Mesa designed by modernist architect Antoine Predock. All the units at La Luz are built with adobe, a mixture of mud and straw and ash, and seem to materialize out of the mesa itself, much like Taos Pueblo or the Great Houses of the Ancestral Puebloans in places like Chaco Canyon. We laugh at our good fortune, because La Luz resembles an updated version of the Taos communes back in the day when Dennis Hopper and friends ran the so-called "Freak Nation." Coincidentally, La Luz celebrated its fiftieth anniversary this year. Construction started in 1968, the same year that launched so many of my generation as *Soixante Huitards*.

While writing this, I decided to try to locate Chantal. I had the crazy idea that I could persuade her to write her own postscript, which would serve as a post mortem of sorts. Why not, given the convenience of online social networking today? So I googled Chantal, and then searched for her on Facebook. My search turned up only one lead: a page on Facebook that fit her profile by name, age, and country. The problem was, this Chantal had created her page ten years before and had not since updated. And instead of a photograph of herself, she had uploaded a photograph of a humor magazine with the likeness of a crazed Frenchman, complete with pencil thin moustache, on the cover. There were no photos, no self-description, no e-dress or other information. Nothing. I sent her a message through Facebook, which went unread for two weeks and then disappeared into cyberspace.

So in a final try I put a notice on the Craigslist page for Strasbourg, France: "*Je cherche une amie de Yugoslavie*, circa 1972." I wanted to know what had become of her and how her life had turned out. I was curious to find out if she had remarried and, if so, been happy in her marriage. And I wanted to wish her well.

Unfortunately, I never heard from Chantal, but I did get several e-mails from someone in Strasbourg named Kelly who more than made up for what she lacked in romance by the directness of her approach: "hey im Kelly and u are pretty hot...wow id seriously fuck the shit out of you."

Though captivated by the pure poetry of her words, I ignored her warm invitation.

But seriously, I can't say her vulgarity surprised me all that much. I mean, let's face it, we're living in a rather crude time, a time when none other than the President of the United States famously remarked that he, too, takes the direct approach: 'Grab 'em by the pussy.'

As Chantal would say, "*C'est fini!*"

—Albuquerque, New Mexico, August 2018

Of This Place
Photographs of the Places that Have Shaped my Life

Cathedral Basilica of Saint Francis of Assisi, Santa Fe, New Mexico, 2018, (photograph by author).

Santa Fe Plaza, 2018 (photograph by author).

Loretto Chapel and Loretto Hotel, Santa Fe, New Mexico, 2018 (photograph by author).

New Mexico Museum of Art, Santa Fe, New Mexico, 2018 (photograph by author).

New Mexico Museum of Art detail, Santa Fe, New Mexico, 2018 (photograph by author).

Chaco Canyon, Pueblo Bonito from above, 2016 (photograph by author).

Chaco Canyon, Pueblo Bonito and ghosts, 2015 (photograph by author).

Chaco Canyon, Chetro Ketl, 2017 (photograph by author).

Chaco Canyon, great kiva at Chetro Ketl, 2017 (photograph by author).

Taos Pueblo, South House, 2013 (photograph by author).

Taos Pueblo, San Geronimo Church, 2013 (photograph by author).

Snow falling on San Francisco de Asis Church, Ranchos de Taos, 2017 (photograph by author).

San Francisco de Asis Church detail, Ranchos de Taos, 2017 (photograph by author).

San Esteban Rey Mission Church, Acoma, 2013 (photograph by author).

Acoma Pueblo ladder, 2013 (photograph by author).

Pedernal, one of Georgia O'Keeffe's favorite subjects, near Abiquiu, New Mexico, 2015 (photograph by author).

Ghosts of Abo Ruin, New Mexico, 2013 (photograph by author).

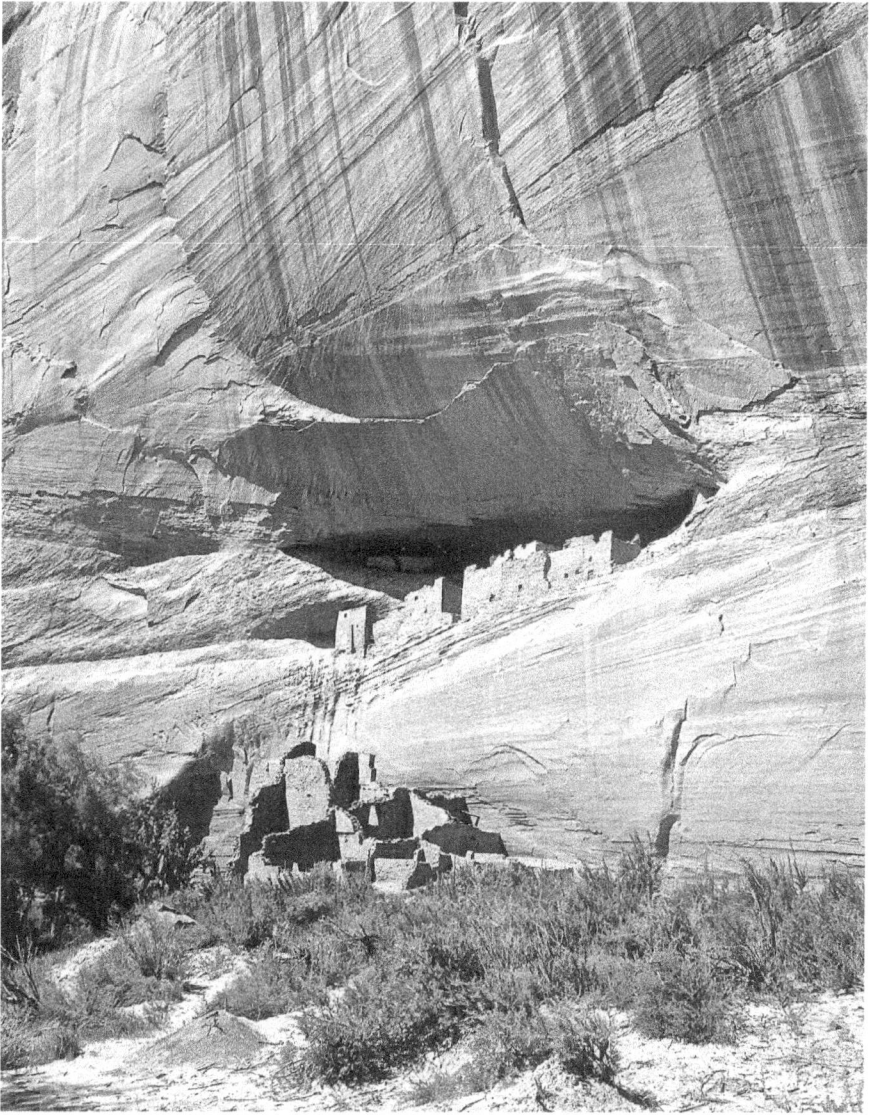

White House Ruin, Canyon de Chelly, Arizona, 1990 (photograph by author).

Zozobra or "Old Man Gloom" moments before he is banished to start the 1990 Santa Fe Fiesta, Santa Fe, New Mexico, 1990, an appropriate end to this improbable, but hopeful, memoir (photograph by author).

Post Dedication

This book is dedicated to Chantal, wherever she is; to Susie, who died of breast cancer in 1978; to Andy, who returned to England and his life as an aristocrat; to Heather, who disappeared much too early from my life; to Joe and Faye, who divorced and went their separate ways; to Dennis and Vicki, who went on to have successful careers in medicine and law respectively; to Alan, who has become a writer of stature and now lives in Vermont in a straw house he built himself; and to Ross, who lives outside Paris with his French wife (not Chantal).

www.ingramcontent.com/pod-product-compliance
Lightning Source LLC
Chambersburg PA
CBHW031436270326
41930CB00007B/738